The
LIBERTY BELL ERA
THE AFRICAN AMERICAN STORY

The Liberty Bell Era:
The African American Story
Text © 2003 by Charles L. Blockson
Photographs and artwork from the Charles L. Blockson
Afro-American Collection
ISBN 1-879441-88-8

Library of Congress Control Number:2003090734

Published by

BOOKS
Harrisburg, PA

Seitz & Seitz, Inc.
1010 North Third Street
Harrisburg, PA 17102
www.celebratePA.com

Designed by Klinginsmith & Company

Printed in China by Regent Publishing Services
St. Louis, MO 63123

The
LIBERTY BELL ERA
THE AFRICAN AMERICAN STORY

CHARLES L. BLOCKSON

CONTENTS

INTRODUCTION

O, let America be America again.
The land that never has been yet;
And yet must be the land where every man is free,
The land that's mine — the poor man's, Indian, Negro's — Me."

Langston Hughes

No matter how you look at it, African people played a major role in American history and culture long before the Liberty Bell, the Declaration of Independence, the Constitution, and the Emancipation Proclamation. The white Founding Fathers revolted against British tyrannical rule and proclaimed that "all men are created equal, that they are endowed by their Creator with certain unalienable rights, that among these rights are life, liberty and the pursuit of happiness." Both enslaved and free African people also believed that all persons were created equal and had certain unalienable rights, even when a large portion of America was notoriously prejudiced and cruel to them.

The soul-stirring words in our leading historical documents were written by the Founding Fathers, many of whom considered themselves Christians. Other prominent whites also expressed their views on liberty and slavery through writing. The theme "to be good and faithful servants in bondage in order to enjoy the great privileges of heaven" was embodied in the catechism and in the Ten Commandments that Cotton Mather, clergyman and historian who led the Salem, Massachusetts, witchcraft trials, wrote for the slaves in 1706. His theme was echoed by other prominent religious leaders.

"This hypocrisy makes the black hate the name of Christian," said Benjamin Coleman, a Quaker minister. In some colonies, the legal status of enslaved Africans was never rigidly formed. Considered both as property and as persons before the law, they could acquire, receive, hold, administer and transfer property, sue or be sued, be tried by grand and petit juries, with the right to pass upon trial jurors, and offer testimony against anyone.

Through the stories in this book, readers will come to know African people who gained prominence in early America, people such as:

Abijah Prince, who in 1774 reportedly owned 100 acres of land in Guilford, Vermont, and was a founder of Sunderland in the same county;

Jethro, a slave who saved the Plymouth colony from annihilation by Native Americans in 1676 and thereby forestalled attacks on other colonies that probably would have led to devastation and withdrawal of Europeans from North America;

York, an enslaved Virginia African American who played a vital role in Lewis and Clark's historic expedition that led them to the Pacific Ocean in 1803. York became the first African American to cross the United States from coast to coast.

Peter Williams, who was purchased as a slave for about $40 by the trustees of the John Street Church in New York City. He worked as the church's first sexton. After

The Rev. Peter Williams, born a slave, purchased by John Aymar, expert cigar maker. Later purchased by New York's John Street Methodist Church and considered the church his master. Was church sexton. Purchased his freedom and repaid the church that bought him. Founded the first African American Church in New York in 1788. Established African American Methodism in New York. Published his oration on the slave trade in 1808.

gaining his freedom, Williams went into the cigar-making business and founded Mother Zion African Methodist Episcopal Church, the first African American church in New York City. Williams became wealthy and was publicized as an American success story. His wife, Molly, a civic-minded woman, became a long-time volunteer firefighter, pulling her favorite engine without assistance.

The institution of human bondage pre-dates the founding of the United States of America. As long as there have been people of power and influence, there also have been people who were denied liberty and the pursuit of happiness. African people were brought to America and held captive against their will. The most important word in America's origin and growth is freedom. Although the Liberty Bell's symbolism rang hollow for some African Americans, they continued to remain loyal to America, while the whole story of slavery and its connection to the Liberty Bell is still untold.

In 1857, the United States Supreme Court handed down a famous decision in the case of an African American slave named Dred Scott, who was taken by his master to live in the free state of Illinois and subsequently to a fort in the northern part of the Louisiana Purchase where slavery had been excluded by the Missouri Compromise. Scott had filed a lawsuit for his freedom, claiming that residence on free soil made him free. The court, denying this, held that Scott could not sue because he was not a citizen. In fact, the court went further to say that a slaveholder could take his slaves anywhere in the territories and still retain title to them.

Although Dred Scott did not receive his freedom from the Supreme Court, other African Americans gained their freedom after the Civil War. The French government recognized the contribution of the enslaved African Americans to this country when in 1884, as a symbol of friendship between the two nations, it gave the Statue of Liberty (its proper name is "Liberty Enlightening the World") to the United States. The original Statue of Liberty, modeled after the image of a woman of African descent, had broken shackles on her feet to symbolize the broken chains of "chattel slavery," but they are seldom seen.

Frederic Auguste Bartholdi, the designer and sculptor of the statue, designed the monument after a suggestion from his friend, internationally known author and writer Victor Hugo, who was an abolitionist and an admirer of John Brown. In recent years historians and scholars have acknowledged the true origin of this national monument.

Based on the trials and achievements of African Americans, this book tells a story that is relevant to all readers. It presents an overall view of the long and gripping history of the African Diaspora before and beyond the Liberty Bell's era. For the most part, people of African descent have been viewed outside the mainstream of American history, rather than as active participants. To the average cultivated reader, African American history and literature suggests the writing of Frederick Douglass, W.E.B. Dubois, Langston Hughes, Alex Haley, Martin Luther King, Alice Walker, and Toni Morrison, all of whom are familiar to most readers in this country.

African American literature is in many ways as rich in ancient tradition as in modern challenges. Janheinz Jahn, a respected Neo-African literature scholar, tells us there were Africans who wrote in hieroglyphics and also some who wrote in Phoenician and Greek script as well as those who later wrote in Arabic and European languages.

Thomas Jefferson once said that, "Slavery is like a fire bell in the night." No one knows when the alarming and terrifying bell will ring, projecting fear and confusion. Even today, the shadow of the peculiar institution of slavery continues to hover over and throughout America. Many of America's most treasured historical monuments, buildings, and national parks are connected to the institution of slavery. They include Independence Hall, The Liberty Bell, The White House, and the Statue of Liberty.

We must remember that it was enslaved Africans who pulled down the statue of King George III in New York City in 1775 during the era of the American Revolution. During the Civil War, slaves hoisted cannons for the Confederate attack on Fort Sumter, South Carolina, that sparked the bloodiest war in our nation's history. Many great colonial mansions and famous antebellum buildings owed their beauty and durability to enslaved African artisans. Probably the most famous national structures built by slave labor were the White House and the Capitol in Washington, D.C.

On December 2, 1863, the *New York Tribune* in an article entitled "The Negro Slave and The Statue of Freedom" said that the statue of freedom on the Capitol at Washington was erected and put in place by a Negro slave, Philip Reed. The article added "a Negro master builder lifted piece by piece, joint by joint, together until they blended into the majestic freedom." A work on the Rotunda and Dome in the Capitol's library gives the name of this slave, the article concluded. All of this is part of the African American story.

I am most grateful to my publisher, Blair Seitz, and to John Hope, my editor, for their patience and meticulous attention to details of the production. I am also grateful to Art Director Cheryl Klinginsmith, the designer of this book and jacket and her care and assiduity, and to Lisa K. Fitch for typing the manuscript and her invaluable suggestions.

This book is respectfully dedicated to the memory of our ancestors, both black and white, who represented the morality of America during our nation's long stormy history.

Charles L. Blockson
Philadelphia, Pennsylvania
August 2002

ONE

BLACK GOLD: THE ECONOMIC FOUNDATION OF THE UNITED STATES

"What would have been the fate of the New World had there been no Africa?"

Jose Antonio Saco – Spanish American Historian

EARLY AFRICA

It is too widely believed that the history of Black Africa merely consists of ignorance, jungle, and an endless series of massacres, petty rulers, and civilizations that never progressed beyond a state of barbarism. Nothing can be further from the truth. Africa's cultural heritage is as old as humankind itself, for it is in Africa that the oldest known human fossils and artifacts have been unearthed. Much of Africa's traditional literature and history is oral; however, people of African descent for thousands of years have written in various languages on almost every conceivable subject, from as early as 1000 A.D., some 300 years after the Mohammedans had invaded Africa.

Even before people of African descent arrived in Jamestown, Virginia, in 1619, other African people had arrived long before on the North American continent. In 1526, with the Spanish colonizers in South Carolina, Africans came as skilled sailors, soldiers, and servants. One of the early explorers, Estevan de Dorantes (Estevanico), was the first person to enter the southwestern part of America. Most of the enslaved African people were not the heathens or savages traditionally portrayed in European and American history books and films; most were part of an advanced culture that had knowledge of iron making.

For instance, the kings of the Ashanti people in Ghana sat on thrones encased in massive gold, enveloped in the richest silks, and wearing as many ornaments of pure gold around their necks, arms, wrists, fingers, and ankles as they comfortably could. White African writer Beryl Markham wrote, "There are as many Africas as there are books written about Africa."

The beginning of humankind was discovered in Mother Africa, a continent of the Queen of Sheba, of Ophis, King Solomon's mines, and Kush, with its splendid capital city of Meroe, where advanced cultures flourished before Christianity was born. Here, too, were the great kingdoms of Ghana and the merchant cities of the East African Coast with a thriving Africa and India trade, and prosperous cities and states of Zimbabwe and Mapungubew. In the Songhay Empire, Mali, a highly developed kingdom, attracted tradesmen and scholars throughout the ancient world seeking knowledge at the University of Sankoree located in the fabled city of Timbuktu.

In 1352, the historian Ibn Batuta visited Mali and found a nearly total black population in which there were numerous lawyers. Subeiman, the king at that time, gave audiences in a hall adorned with silver plaques. One African scholar wrote that in this city were great stores of doctors, judges, priests, and other charges. There were other important kingdoms such as Dahomey, Yoruba, Mandingo, Igbo, and the Congo.

For centuries, the so-called "Dark Continent" was known by Europeans as a continent of great wealth. In the ancient city of Benin in Nigeria, Africa's largest country, for more than 500 years, artists created objects in brass, ivory, terracotta, and wood for use in divine kingship and queenship rituals, to adorn the royal palaces, and to honor the king and queen mothers, chiefs, warriors, and other prominent officials of the court. Some scholars wrote that the royal Benin bronze sculptures rival the sculptures of ancient Greece and Rome.

The African Diaspora into the European colonies most probably began with the discovery of the New World by the first European navigator, Christopher Columbus. On the *Santa Maria*, one of Columbus' crewmen, Pedro Alonzo Niño, has been identified as a sailor of African descent. Without a doubt other African seamen and explorers accompanied the Spanish explorers Balboa, Ponce de Leon, Cortez, Pizarro, and Menendez on their travels and explorations. In 1538, Estevanico, an African explorer representing Spain, led an expedition from Mexico into the territory of the North American southwest. Estevanico is credited with the discovery of what are now Arizona and New Mexico. Some historical records have suggested that African sailors were trading among the indigenous people of Central and South America several decades before Columbus.

English historian Basil Davidson wrote, "Between the 15th and 19th centuries the African continent earned the name 'Black Mother,' because of its seemingly inexhaustible supply of humanity to work the mines and plantations of the Western Hemisphere." In 1562, Britain entered the cruel commerce of the slave trade when Sir John Hawkins sold a large cargo of African captives to Spanish planters on the Caribbean Island of Hispaniola (Haiti). Though Queen Elizabeth permitted Hawkins to include the figure of a bound African in his coat of arms, she denied Hawkins the right to transport slaves from Africa. Hawkins later convinced the Queen to give him seven slave ships; one, called Jesus, was caught in a storm in the Caribbean with a cargo of slaves and went down in 1595.

The demands of European consumers for New World crops and goods helped fuel the slave trade, following a triangular route between Africa, the Caribbean, North America, and Europe. Slave traders from Denmark, Holland, Portugal, Spain, France, and England delivered African captives in exchange for products such as rum, sugar, and tobacco that European consumers wanted. Eventually, the trading route also distributed Virginia tobacco, New England rum and indigo, cotton, and rice crops from South Carolina and Georgia.

Enslaved men, women, and children lived in constant fear of the brutal treatment administered by the hands of American slave owners, and were in constant fear of being sold away from their loved ones. Enslaved women often experienced sexual exploitation at the hands of overseers and slave owners. However, no event was more traumatic in the lives of enslaved bonds people than that of forcible separation from their families.

Sometimes enslaved Africans betrayed their countrymen. Berenhead and Peter were informers for their slave master; Berenhead, in Gloucester County, Virginia in 1663, and Peter at the Parish of St. John in South Carolina in 1740. A slave named Cato led another revolt on the Stono plantation in South Carolina in 1734. On July 2, 1822, Telemarque, otherwise known to history as Denmark Vesey, was hanged for plotting the largest slave insurrection in history from Charleston, South Carolina. Mark and Phillis of Charleston, South Carolina, killed their master "to move things along," after learning that he had made provisions for liberation of his slaves upon his death. Mark was hanged in 1775 for the crime and Phillis was burned alive.

The most sensational and successful slave revolt occurred in August 1831 in Southampton, Virginia. A trusted slave named

Nat Turner plotted the most sensational slave revolt in American history. Some 57 to 60 whites were killed by Turner and his men. And 40 more blacks were killed in response at Southampton, Virginia, in 1831.

Nat Turner led the revolt with 70 followers, murdering 53 white men, women, and children, before he and his followers were captured. Turner and some of the others were tried and hanged.

The enslavement of Africans did not begin with the Europeans; it began earlier in the eighth century with the Muslims and Arabs, and even among some African states. When Europeans discovered the vast wealth that could be accumulated from the slave trade, they established slave trading "coffles" throughout West Africa. Historians estimate as many as 10,000 slaves a year passed through the bleak fortresses. Slavery among Africans themselves was different from the European slave traders in that they usually kept families together and permitted marriages between slaves owners and their captives.

White European and American slave owners attempted to justify enslavement of Africans, who they viewed as uncivilized beings, and quoted scriptures from the Bible to defend their position on enslavement of African people. Many African kings, queens, and chiefs did not sit idly by watching white invaders enslave their subjects. Ann Zingha, famous Amazon Queen of Matamba, West Africa, who lived from 1582 to 1663, led her army of fierce women warriors against Portuguese and other European slave hunters. She won battle after battle. Other African rulers continued to repel invading European slave hunters for centuries after this legendary woman's death.

The Atlantic slave trade started out on a small scale and grew in scope in America following the events that brought the first "twenty odd Negroes" to Jamestown, Virginia. Anthony Johnson and his wife, Mary, gave birth to a son named Anthony, after his father. He was the first African child baptized a Christian in America. The American colonists soon found tobacco to be a profitable export crop and the demand for more slaves increased. As planters farmed more land in the south, the colonies turned their attention to the cultivation of sugar, rice, cotton, and indigo.

By the late 1700s, busy slave markets had been established in northern colonies. Later in the century, the call for liberty and independence in the 13 colonies was sounded by whites and enslaved Africans people. The white colonists sought freedom from their British oppressors, while African people sought freedom from their white oppressors. Both groups reached a climax in the era of the American Revolution.

In this book, the City of Philadelphia is given a dominant role. Philadelphia was not only one of the most important of American cities, it also was one of the historic cities during the colonial period. It is a "shrine city," for here is Independence Hall and the Liberty Bell that have become international symbols because of their association with many different struggles for freedom. Philadelphia's narrow streets once echoed with the footsteps of George Washington, Thomas Jefferson, Benjamin Franklin, Alexander Hamilton, Betsy Ross, Thomas Paine, and many other prominent men and women who were involved in the dramatic and turbulent course of American history. Upon those cobblestone streets also walked African American freedom seekers such as Richard Allen, Absalom Jones, James Forten, Frederick Douglass, Sojourner Truth, and Harriet Tubman.

Thomas Paine, born in England, signer of the Declaration of Independence, known primarily for his radical ideas. Author of "Common Sense," he published the poetry of Phillis Wheatley in Philadelphia. He was a member of the Pennsylvania Abolition Society.

16

Frederick Douglass, a rebellious Maryland slave, often suffered because of his indomitable spirit. In 1838, when he was 21 years old, he escaped to New Bedford, Massachusetts, learned to read and write, married, and changed his name. He became a skilled abolitionist speaker. His print shop in Rochester, New York, was a depot on the Underground Railroad. During the Civil War, he encouraged African Americans to enlist in the Union Army. Two of Douglass' sons served with the celebrated 54th Colored Infantry Regiment.

Philadelphia was the largest and the most important American city. Here the First and the Second Continental Congresses met; however, the political, economic and social privileges gained by white Americans were disallowed for African Americans in the new nation. The war for American Independence had been won, yet the war for equality for African Americans had just begun. The story of the Liberty Bell and the story of Betsy Ross and the flag have been recounted so many times in history books that most American know their stories by heart. Yet most Americans do not know the major contributions to our history by people of African descent.

Most American students can quote the soul stirring patriotic statement said by Revolutionary War hero Nathan Hale: "I regret that I have but one life to give to my country." However, very few Americans know that when the British hung Hale on September 22, 1776, as an American spy, he was hanged by a former slave named Bill Richmond. After the war, while living in England, Richmond became that country's heavyweight boxing champion.

Moreover, most Americans do not know that on October 4, 1777, Samuel Charlton, a 17-year-old slave who enlisted as his master's substitute, was one of the African American soldiers fighting in the daring attack on the British at the Battle of Germantown, or that Catto Carlile and Scipio, Africans free born from New England coastal towns, enlisted for service under Captain John Paul Jones. African Americans who knew the seas, whether they were free or enslaved, were welcomed in the Continental Navy.

Most American whites and blacks are victims of a mis-education, a form of ignorance that in many ways represents the worst form of slavery. There is in America today a lack of understanding that breeds fear, suspicion, hate, insecurity, and inferiority, evils that detract from us as civilized beings. An understanding of the past may add an understanding of the present. Inconsistency

Bill Richmond, a 15-year-old African American boy who was the hangman at Nathan Hale's execution on September 22, 1776. Richmond later became heavyweight boxing champion of England.

in the application of knowledge has become the basic cause of conflict between the races.

I believe that various races can work together and walk upon this earth in brotherhood and sisterhood. The United States Secretary of State, Colin Powell, believes it too. On the Fourth of July 2002, Colin Powell received The Liberty Medal in Philadelphia. Powell, the son of Jamaican immigrants who grew up in New York City, stood in front of Independence Hall and declared in his acceptance speech, "We hold these truths to be self-evident, that all men are created equal. Thirteen words for thirteen colonies. Thirteen words that 226 years later still throw the light of hope to the darkest corners of tyranny and oppression." He added, "If I had been around at the time, I probably would have been regarded as property, not as a man. But the fact that I hold public office is evidence of the nation's continuing progress."

In the pages of this book you will meet and come to know major and minor personalities in a dramatic and too little known chapter in American history. You'll learn of the life of ordinary citizens, who they were, where they lived, and what they did. The book includes photographs, paintings, broadsides, drawings, woodcuts, letters, posters, handbills, and pamphlets, many never before seen by the public. All footnotes have been left out of this book, under the impression that they annoy readers more than they help. I have cited sources throughout the book and included other sources in the bibliography.

I want to make it clear to readers that this book is not a product of imagination or fiction. Did George Washington ever tell a lie? Or did Betsy Ross make the first American flag? Some modern historians believe that the 13-star Old Glory may not have been made by Betsy Ross, but instead was designed by Francis Hopkinson, a signer of the Declaration of Independence.

TWO

ENSLAVED AFRICANS IN THE CITY OF BROTHERLY LOVE

Philadelphia – a group of African Americans in front of the Bank of Pennsylvania (from 1814 water color by Pavel Petrovich Svinin), courtesy of the Roger Fund, Metropolitan Museum of Art, New York.

While the European settlers who came to Pennsylvania identified with William Penn's dream of a free society, the guarantees of liberty they formulated were limited to white men. Peaceful relations with the Native Americans, a feature of early colonial life, did not last; white settlers pushed farther and farther west, claiming as their own the territories they entered. By the time of the Declaration of Independence, the Native Americans had yielded most of their land in Pennsylvania.

Perhaps it was the shared experience of exploitation that led to the interaction of people of African descent and Native Americans here as in other states. Native Americans gave refuge to enslaved runaway Africans, often adopting them into community life and frequently intermarrying. The enslavement of people of African descent was intimately related to the history of Native Americans, as it was also related to European Americans. The economical development of colonial and ante-bellum Philadelphia was partly subsidized by the "peculiar" institution of slavery. Transplanted Africans maintained a vocabulary and means of expression preserved from the African tradition that was completely foreign to whites. Many of the captive Africans resisted enslavement at every step in their forced relocation. Even those who did not run away often were obstinate or uncooperative workers.

Throughout the colonial period and into the era of the Revolution, many captive Africans in Philadelphia and elsewhere were sometime called Guineas (taken from the name of a coin). This term applied to those who were taken from the Guinea Coast or Gold Coast in West Africa. The names Guineatown, Guinea Hill, or Guinea Run can still be found in various areas of Pennsylvania and throughout the eastern seacoast.

Africans were present among the earliest settlers in Pennsylvania, some of whom were here as early as 1639. They arrived with the Dutch and Swedish settlers. In April 1639, a Swedish ship, the *Vogel Grip*, returned from the Caribbean with a slave named Anthony and docked in Delaware, then known as New Sweden. Anthony served as a slave under the governor of New Sweden, John Printz, who moved his government from Fort Christiana to Tinicum Island, near the present site of the Philadelphia Airport. Anthony holds the distinction of possibly being the first person of African descent in present day Pennsylvania.

When William Penn, the English Quaker, arrived in the colony that bears his name in 1682, he declared that his colony should be a place of complete religious and racial freedom, of universal goodwill, and of fine and thrifty citizenship. Penn's own name for his city was the "Holy Experiment." Shortly after he arrived in his colony, Penn employed Lasse Cock, an important Swedish agent, who served as his interpreter to the Lenni Lenape, a local Native American tribe. Cock was also a slave owner.

Although Penn was known for his political and religious liberalism, he permitted human slavery to blemish his liberal vision. The Quaker founder of the Commonwealth of Pennsylvania and his family owned slaves named Peter, Sam, Sue, Dorcas, Hesia, Yass, Jack, and Jack's wife, Parthenia. When Penn made his first return trip to England in 1684, he stated in his will that his five slaves "Mingo, Wissen, Julius, Maria and Sarah to be hired out." In 1701, Penn, on his return to England, liberated his slaves, stating, "I give to …my blacks their freedom as is under my hand already." This will, which was left with James Logan, Penn's secretary, was not carried out. Penn's last will contains no mention of his blacks. Logan and the other administrators stated that they could not follow Penn's instructions because they were a "private matter."

In the 1701 will, he gave one of his slaves, "Old Sam," and his children, forever, 100 acres of land. But this will was invalidated by a later one in which there is no mention of Old Sam or his children. The 1701 will was the first official record of African American property ownership in Pennsylvania.

Historians in the past and present have unjustly written that slavery in Pennsylvania was not as severe or harsh as slavery in the south. The reality is that the act of slavery is unjust and inhumane no matter where it existed or how well or cruelly a slave is treated. Both the Declaration of Independence and the Liberty Bell had noble words of equality for all men, but neither, nor the American Revolutionary War, was designed to bring equality or freedom to freed or enslaved African Americans.

By the middle of the 16th century, more than 10,000 enslaved Africans a year were being sold to European colonists in the West Indies. The enslaved Africans generally did not come directly from Africa, but from the British West Indies, where they underwent a conditioning or seasoning process before being sent to Pennsylvania through the Port of Philadelphia. Most of these imported Africans originally came from West Africa, occasionally called the Gold Coast or the Guinea Coast.

Slave ships, or "Ships of Sorrow" as they were often called, took many weeks to traverse the Atlantic Ocean during the Middle

Passage — the distance between Africa and the New World. During the long voyage, many slaves died or committed suicide by jumping overboard into the shark-infested ocean. They were stacked like logwood in dank holes, chained together, and permitted on deck only for a short time per day for fresh air and exercise. During a violent storm they got neither. The food was often unfit to digest, often spoiled, and the water stagnant. Their quarters were filthy. For each five slaves delivered safely in America, scholars estimate that one perished. Those who rebelled often met a violent death on shipboard.

The number of enslaved Africans in Pennsylvania was never large compared to those held in captivity in Southern colonies. For enslaved Africans, newly arrived and huddled in fright in a strange world, the quest to survive was all they had. Upon arriving in Philadelphia and other colonial ports, enslaved Africans were forced to smear their bodies with oil that coated the sores and other abrasions from chains. The oil also gave their bodies a healthy glistening look so that they would be bought for higher prices. Philadelphia's enslaved Africans were generally housed in their owners' homes and employed as domestic servants without pay.

Whenever a slave ship arrived in Colonial Philadelphia, along the area of the Delaware River known today as Penn's Landing, its arrival was announced by a town crier, or advertised in the local newspapers. For about a century prior to the Revolutionary War, the slave trade thrived as a readily accepted enterprise in colonial America and elsewhere. Even the famed *Mayflower* that brought the pilgrims, a small group of English set-

LEFT: *Shown here is a group of enslaved African people on one of the Caribbean Islands. Here they underwent a "seasoning" or what some historians called a "conditioning process" before being sent to the American colonies.*

tlers, to Plymouth, Massachusetts, in 1620, was connected with the institution of slavery. The first plan for self-government in America, called the Mayflower Compact, was signed aboard that ship. Some scholars write that the *Mayflower* was a former slave ship. Much speculation has been spent on the identification of the *Mayflower*. A ship of 180 tons burden, it presumably resembled other ships of the period and bore a name common to other vessels. Among the more conspicuous speculation is that the *Mayflower* was a former slave ship and that its captain, Christopher Jones, was a pirate and thief who had been released from prison to lead the voyage from Southampton, England, for America.

In Philadelphia, ships anchored in the Delaware River were christened with names such as the *Isabella* and the *Charming Sally*, a schooner that brought enslaved Africans from the River Gambia. Quaker and non-Quaker merchants were part of Philadelphia's money-making business who traded in rum, sugar, molasses, silver, Negroes, salt, and wine to accumulate wealth and power.

RUNAWAY SLAVE ADVERTISEMENTS

The woman was very adverse to going, gave me the slip, I shall dispose of her as soon as I can, for she has played some ill pranks in the family.

Quaker slaveholder Isaac Norris to a Maryland slave buyer

Shown here is an early image of a runaway slave woman.

26

Early newspaper advertising slaves to be sold — a choice cargo of about 250 fine and healthy Negroes.

Enslaved Africans were constantly and understandably seeking freedom by running away from their owners. The *American Weekly Mercury*, the first newspaper printed in Philadelphia in the year 1719, advertised in its second issue that a bright mulatto by the name of Johnny had run away. The following are some ads as they appeared in the newspapers.

January 31, 1721–For Sale Female Slave

A very likely Negro woman to be sold, aged about 28 years. Fit for country or city business. She can card, spin, knit and milk; and any other country work. Whoever has a mind for the said Negro report to Andrew Bradford in Philadelphia. The *American Weekly Mercury* (Philadelphia)

February 20, 1776 – Forty Shillings Reward

Run away, last Thursday evening, from the subscriber living on Second Street near Market Street, a Negro woman named Hannah, about 22 years old. A stout-made, hearty girl, full faced, about rather down countenance, scare on her cheeks (the mark of her tribe in Guinea) had only her work clothes on being a green baize short gown, stripped lacey petticoat, an old pair of men's shoes and stocking, a plain linen cap. Whoever will bring said Negro woman to her master, shall have above reward and reasonable charges. Robert Cospar. It is supposed that she is lurking in town as she has been seen since she went off.

In *The Pennsylvania Packet*, May 1, 1784,
the following notice appeared:

John Letelier – Eight dollars reward. Ran away from the subscriber, a Negro named John Frances by trade a goldsmith. Said Negro was carried to New York and left in charge of Ephraim Brasher, goldsmith, from who he absconded, and returned to me — whoever takes up said Negro and delivers him to John Letilier, goldsmith in Market Street, or to the subscriber in New York, shall have the above reward and all reasonable charge paid.

SLAVES FOR SALE IN SOCIETY HILL

Throughout colonial Philadelphia, Africans were often viewed as sub-human, mankind's lowest species. Some whites thought slavery was a shame and an outrage and attempted to do something about it. A number of enslaved Africans brought in chains to the city died from the cold weather; some often arrived naked at the docks located along Penn's Landing. One benevolent Quaker said of one enslaved woman that, "I have put her on clothes. It not being the custom for them to go naked, people will not buy them so."

As strange as it may seem, slaves were sold a short distance from the Liberty Bell and Independence Hall, on Water Street between Spruce and High, now known as Market Street. Buyers were permitted to pull limbs and examine their goods, who were

Shown here is a group of enslaved African people being sold at auction. Slaves were property and could be displayed and examined shamefully before being sold to a buyer.

usually completely naked. Slaves that were not sold immediately were put into compounds until a buyer could be found. These compounds were fenced off rectangles and were located not far from the auction area.

A Pennsylvania State Historical Marker, located at Two South Front Street, marks the site of the London Coffee House, where a slave auction block once stood. Built in 1702 by Charles Reed, who obtained the land from William Penn's daughter Laetitia, the coffee house featured a platform on which enslaved Africans were displayed and sold. In 1754, William Bradford established the building as a meeting place for merchants and sea captains. In the back of the building, the *Pennsylvania Journal* was printed and sold. Bradford also owned slaves.

During colonial times, the whipping post, the stocks, and the pillory were located at Second and High Streets. African Americans as well as whites were punished for theft and other crimes here. Candidates for punishment at the whipping post were named by the court. The Court of Quarter Sessions on July 4, 1693, stated, "The Constable of Philadelphia or any other person whatsoever was given power to take up Negroes, male or female, whom they should gather about the first days of the week, without a pass from their Mr. or Mrs. [master or mistress], or not in their company, and carry them to the gallows, there remain that night, and that without meat or drink, and to cause them to be publickly whipped the next morning with 39 lashes well laid on their backs, for which their said Mr. or Mrs. should pay 15 [cents] to the shipper at his delivery of them to his owner."

Shipping Records

The ships that brought enslaved Africans to the City of Brotherly Love were generally owned by a small number of wealthy merchants who dispatched them, or by independent shippers commissioned by the merchants. To accommodate their lucrative enterprise, a merchant ship had to be furnished with proper fittings and tackle.

Philadelphia was a foremost shipbuilding center and for Philadelphia merchants, ships could be converted at little expense or loss of time. If the sailing ships were scheduled to sail to Africa, conversion would take longer, since facilities for longer cargo would be needed. Shippers throughout the colonies came to Philadelphia to convert a sloop or schooner into a slave ship. Laden with valuable human cargo, slave ship captains often sailed for the American colonies, pre-scheduling embarkation so that they would return during the early spring's favorable months for slave trading. Because of fears of mutiny and other forms of revolts, slaves were kept in shackles in the hold, guarded until the sight of Africa was lost on the horizon.

Several insurance companies in Philadelphia were established to protect Philadelphia ship owners against loss from storms and pirates, privateers from foreign countries who preyed on the

An early engraving showing enslaved Africans being brought abroad a slave ship

Atlantic Ocean and the Caribbean Islands. For freed people of African descent, there was some hope in bringing about a movement towards freedom that was the contribution of abolitionists. For example, in January 1800, the United States Congress rejected a petition sent by 74 freed African Americans from Philadelphia asking that body for the abolition of slavery. The petition was rejected 85-1. It was the first petition by African Americans to Congress in America.

The first marine insurance company in the United States, the Insurance Company of North America, was founded in Philadelphia in 1792. It is also the oldest American stock insurance company. According to the official Insurance Company of North America history, its customers included prominent Philadelphia merchant and ship owner Stephen Girard, one of America's wealthiest men of his day. According to his will, Girard owned plantations and slaves near New Orleans. The record books also show that the company insured cargoes between Caribbean slave ports such as San Dominique (Haiti) and New Orleans, and between Virginia and other sugar plantation colonies in Barbados and Martinique. The company also had an agent in the enslaved island of Jamaica as early as 1797.

The company was one of the leading insurers of maritime trade in the British West Indies. Insurance companies also insured items produced from slave labor such as coffee, fish, flour, rum, and sugar. Historical documents reveal that some insurance companies did not enter into insurance agreements as specific items of policy; however, slaves were hidden among other ship cargo, which is now called "fraudulent concealment." The merchants were concerned with protecting their investment — the healthier the slave cargo, the lower the voyage mortality rate and the higher the profits. Entries in most shipping logs gave the names of ship captains, number of ships, African captives, and islands where enslaved Africans were transshipped.

PROMINENT PHILADELPHIA SLAVE
TRADERS AND OWNERS

Many prominent Philadelphia merchants and religious and political figures were involved in the slave trade. The merchants who brought enslaved Africans were the moneyed minority controlling most of the wealth and owning much of the real estate in the Philadelphia area; some of their descendants reside in the area today. Many of these slave-trading families had as many as six ships sailing the Atlantic Ocean at one time. As early as 1684, a slave ship from Bristol, England, sold its cargo of 150 enslaved Africans to eager Philadelphia buyers.

Among the slave traders were Samuel Carpenter, John Dickinson, James Claypoole, Benjamin Mifflin, Samuel Powell, Jr., and John Reynell. The last two were among the wealthiest Quakers in Philadelphia. Also included in this group was the Isaac Norris family for whom Norristown, the county seat of Montgomery County, is named. James Logan, William Penn's secretary, owned slaves. He was one of the most influential Quaker leaders in the colony. Another Quaker, John Bartram, colonial America's botanical genius, owned a slave helper by the name of Harvey. Some writers called Harvey a servant.

Charles Wilson Peale, a non-Quaker, one of the most popular and successful portrait painters in colonial America who painted the now famous portrait of George Washington in 1779, owned a slave named Moses Williams. Williams, who contributed to the development of the fine arts in Philadelphia, was an expert silhouette maker. With money he made from his silhouette proficiency, Williams was able to purchase his freedom.

George McCall, whose family had arrived in the colony around 1680 from Scotland, traded aggressively with the West Indies and advertised in the *Pennsylvania Gazette* and other Philadelphia newspapers that his ships were bringing enslaved

Africans with his two sons, Samuel and Archibald. The house of McCall was a reliable procurer of captive Africans spanning a period from 1718 to 1750. McCall's daughter, Catherine, married a Philadelphia entrepreneur, John Inglis, who also had a pre-occupation with the slave trade. Inglis joined the commercial firm of Willing and Morris. Another of McCall's daughters, Mary, married William Plumstead, who like his father-in-law became a prominent Philadelphia merchant serving Philadelphia as mayor and later as a jurist.

Plumstead renounced his membership in the Society of Friends in order to continue his slave trading activities unharrassed. Plumstead along with his father-in-law and brothers-in-law once owned most of what is now Montgomery County, and was responsible for financing and erecting old St. Peter's Church at Third and Pine Streets. Plumstead also owned large areas of land in Bucks County, northeast of Philadelphia. When an act against the importation of slaves was passed in 1761, many Philadelphia merchants protested, stating that the region had to import slaves to keep the price of labor and therefore the price of staples low. Samuel Mifflin traded in the Philadelphia area around this time and together with his partner Philip Kearney is reported to have made more slaving voyages than any other commercial business. Mifflin was the cousin of Thomas Mifflin, Pennsylvania's first governor.

Robert Meade is reported to have been the only prominent Catholic slave-trading merchant during this era. His two sons, George and Garrett, continued the business after their father's death, engaging in the profitable trade well into the 1770s, when slave trading in Pennsylvania had become unpopular among many citizens. General George G. Meade, the Union hero who decisively held off confederate General Robert Lee at Gettysburg during the Civil War, was the great-great-grandson of George G. Meade.

Few persons in the north spoke kindly of Pierce Butler, a wealthy Georgia-born Philadelphian. Butler inherited his family's large plantation in Georgia while living in Philadelphia. The stock market crash of 1857-1858 forced him to sell his share of slaves in order to pay his debts a few years before the Civil War. A total of 429 enslaved men, women, and children were sold from the auction block for $303,850. The highest value, $1,350, was placed upon a 40-year-old plantation blacksmith, followed by $1,300 for a much younger carpenter. Two older bricklayers, 64 and 70, were deemed worthless. It was a cold business. Butler gave one whole dollar in new quarters to each slave who had been sold. His British actress wife, Fanny Kemble, known for her anti-slavery sentiment while living in Philadelphia, had divorced Butler before the sale of his slaves. It was one of the largest slave sales in the South.

British actress Fanny Kemble was devoted to her husband, Pierce Butler, a wealthy Georgia-born plantation owner who lived in Philadelphia. Kemble became an abolitionist and wrote a famous book about the lives of slaves on her former husband's Georgia plantation.

Joseph Turner became one of the original trustees of what is now the University of Pennsylvania, with his partner William Allen. The company of Allen and Turner was responsible for importing more slaves into Philadelphia than any other merchant company save Willing and Morris. The Van Pelts, direct descendants of Turner, are still living in the Philadelphia area today. Benedict Arnold, hero and traitor of the Revolutionary War, owned a 23-year-old slave named Punch.

Peter Baynton, a merchant, imported slaves, a practice continued by his son, John, a partner in the prosperous firm of Baynton, Wharton and Morgan. Located in the archives of the Pennsylvania Historical and Museum Commission in Harrisburg is a ledger that records the expenses incurred in hiring out a black slave as a sailor. Included among Philadelphia influential slave-holding families were the Cadwaladers, Whartons, Markoes, Shutes, Wisters and Chews. John Dickinson freed more than 50 slaves, but immediately indentured them and held them in captivity on his Dover, Delaware, plantation.

Among the names of other pre-Revolutionary merchants who made a profit from the slave trade were Robert Ellis, John Fuller, John St. Clair, William Frampton, Joseph Sims, William Rodman, Samuel Oldman, Thomas Riche, Thomas Gilbert, Alexander Woodrup, and William Vaughn.

The African Insurance Company of Philadelphia opened an office at 159 Lombard Street in 1810. It was the first insurance company operated by people of African descent in the United States. The first president was Joseph Randolph; Cyrus Porter was treasure and William Coleman was secretary with a capital of $5,000 in $50.00 shares. There is good reason to believe that they did not insure enslaved Africans. The durability of its years of existence is unknown.

WILLINGS ALLEY

Located on Second Street below Walnut Street is Willings Alley, named for Thomas Willings, a prominent Quaker slave-holder who, with his Swedish father-in-law, Andrew Justison, developed Willington, now Wilmington, Delaware, between 1730

Robert Morris, signer of the Declaration of Independence, major financier of the Revolutionary War and Quaker slave trader.

and 1735. The firm of his son, Charles Willings, and Quaker Robert Morris was one of Pennsylvania's most persistent participants in the commerce of slaves between 1754 and 1766.

THE OLD SLAVE MARKET

Formerly on Water between Spruce and Market Streets, (during the colonial period, Market Street was called High Street and Water Street was located at the present area of Penn's Landing), Philadelphia's slave auction block was located in the section that is now called "Olde City." Prospective buyers came to the auction area to examine human cargo. If slaves were clothed in tattered rags, they were an oddity. More often, they were completely naked. Buyers were permitted to pull their limbs and examine them in the most intimate places to check for disease or disability. Those slaves not immediately sold were put in compounds until buyers could be found.

After the enslaved Africans were purchased, they were taken away, separated from any relative and from persons from their former native community in Africa. Suicide was not uncommon. The enslaved Africans were susceptible to smallpox, the flux, dropsy, and rape. Of the survivors of the miserable Middle Passage, very few arrived fit for immediate labor. They were called Guineas because they were largely from the West Coast of Africa. Once the largest unit in English currency, the gold in the Guinea also came from West Africa.

In 1736, the ship *Charming Sally* arrived in Philadelphia, and on the day she was expected, the following advertisement appeared in the Pennsylvania Gazette: "A parcel of likely Negroes Boy's and Girls just arrived on the sloop Charming Sally to be sold ready money, flour or wheat."

The sale itself was the most traumatic form of family separation for enslaved Africans. However, on a few occasions there were moments of joy. In the year 1800, an American ship of war, the *Ganges*, captured two vessels engaged in slavery and brought them to the Port of Philadelphia along the Delaware River. One of the slave vessels had 118 enslaved captives and the other 16 captive Africans. When disembarking for the benefit of fresh air and physical examinations, a husband and wife, separated in the ships, never expecting to meet again, recognized each other. Their mutual recognition was a passionate moment of happiness. The sudden surprise and joy was too powerful for the wife and she became a premature mother. But through assistance from members of the Pennsylvania Abolition Society, the woman was medically aided and given freedom.

The Pennsylvania Abolition Society eventually acquired freedom for all of the enslaved Africans. In appreciation to the *Ganges*, a large number of the former enslaved Africans adopted Ganges as their surname. One man, Harry Ganges, who was freed on October 8, 1800, was indentured to work for a man in

Philadelphia. There are numerous descendants of the *Ganges* captives living in Philadelphia and surrounding areas today. For many years, the descendants of the *Ganges* held reunions in remembrance of their ancestors.

THE GRADUAL ACT OF EMANCIPATION 1780

George Bryan, an eminent Philadelphia Presbyterian lawyer and supporter of the Constitution of 1776, also became the chief sponsor of the Abolition Act. In these years, the Pennsylvania legislature had passed a bill calling for the gradual abolition of slavery, an omen full of promise. On that occasion, two prominent Pennsylvanians were active, Benjamin Franklin and Thomas Paine.

Although Pennsylvania became the first state in the union to abolish slavery, not a single slave went free. The law also forbade bringing any new slaves into the state. A slave child born after the law took effect was to be freed at age 28, giving the master time to recoup the expense of raising a child.

Benjamin Franklin, signer of the Declaration of Independence, printer, author, inventor, philosopher, diplomat, slave owner, and president of the Pennsylvania Abolition Society.

Many captives were unlawfully held in bondage in Philadelphia as late as the 1840s. Many runaway enslaved Africans who came to Pennsylvania were often returned to bondage. When finally passed on March 1, 1780, the new law provided that all children born to slaves after its passage were to become free after a period of indentureship. All slaves who had been born before the passage of the act were to be registered by their masters with the courts, and those not registered by November 1, 1780, were to be freed. At the same time, the colonial black codes, which included a provision against marriage between blacks and whites, were repealed. The Pennsylvania Assembly passed the first state law in America providing for the emancipation of slaves.

Bryan, who drafted the preamble, requested that the wording be engraved on his tombstone. It has been estimated that there were about 6,000 slaves in Pennsylvania in 1780.

THE PENNSYLVANIA ABOLITION SOCIETY

Founded at the Sun Tavern in Philadelphia in 1775 by Quakers and others as the Society for the Relief of Free Negroes Unlawfully Held in Bondage, the Pennsylvania Abolition Society is important not because of its age but because it is the first civic-minded organization in American history where whites and African Americans worked together struggling to gain ends that were not tainted by profit or greed or imagined superiority or inferiority. Because of the turmoil of the American Revolution, the founders didn't meet again as a society until peace had come.

Of the 24 white men elected in 1775, only 10 reappeared in 1784, but within a few weeks the membership rose to 40. Listed among its members were such non-Quakers as Benjamin Franklin, Dr. Benjamin Rush, Thomas Paine, Anthony Benezet, the Marquis de Lafayette, Tench Coxe and Dr. Julian Francis Le Moyne. The society raised money to buy freedom for enslaved Africans, assisted freed slaves in finding employment, gave legal aid to blacks who had been kidnapped into slavery, and fought against proposals introduced into the legislature by pro-slavery forces (including one that would have banished all free African Americans.)

General George Washington owned 317 slaves on his Virginia plantation, Mt. Vernon. He became commander of the Continental Army during the Revolutionary War and later the first President of the United States.

The society also corresponded with antislavery groups throughout the world. Evidently there were loopholes in the society's quest for total abolition. When President George Washington brought some of his slaves when he lived in Philadelphia in the 1790s while serving as president of the United States, he was permitted to house some of them. African Americans and women did not become members of the society until after the Civil War.

Noted anti-slavery and Underground Railroad advocates such as William Still, Robert Purvis, and Quaker Lucretia Mott were included. Today the society continues to spend a large portion of its income on education and to eliminate racial prejudice in many ways.

INDEPENDENCE HALL AND MALL

On Chestnut Street between Fifth and Sixth Streets is Independence Hall, perhaps the most historic landmark in the United States. This historic building was completed in 1734. Both freed and enslaved Africans participated as workmen in the erection of this historic landmark. In 1775, American patriots met here to form the Second Continental Congress. Philadelphia was the seat of the national government from 1775 to 1789. In 1790, it again became national capital, retaining that distinction until the seat of government moved to Washington, D.C., in 1800.

During those years, Independence Hall figured largely in the events that shaped our nation. Here, George Washington was chosen Commander in Chief of the Continental Army. Here on July 4, 1776, the Declaration of Independence was signed. Yet, for all their nobility, the two documents that most Americans associate closely with Independence Hall, the Declaration of Independence and the Constitution, are full of contradictions when applied to African Americans.

The Declaration of Independence is a brilliantly written statement that is quoted repeatedly, but "all men are created equal" is a phrase that gives no comfort for people of African descent. Its principal author, Thomas Jefferson, is an enigma concerning slavery.

Although he condemned King George III for condoning the slave trade, (a section that was deleted by the signers of the

Thomas Jefferson, slaveholder, signer of the Declaration of Independence, statesman and third President of the United States.

Declaration), Jefferson continued as a slave owner himself. Many of the distinguished signers of that historic document were slave owners. The Constitution avoids any direct mention of slavery. In fact, slavery was not named in it until the passage of the 13th Amendment.

However, the Constitution provided slavery with the basis it needed to survive and flourish. A significant part of that support was the three-fifths compromise, which meant that, for census purposes, each slave would be counted as three-fifths of a person. As a result, it allowed slave states to send representatives to Congress based on their black populations. There was opposition to their stance: firebrand Thomas Paine thought that the Continental Congress should declare the abolition of slavery as an objective, but he met opposition. In fact, by the time of the Civil War, 11 out of 16 presidents, 17 out of 28 Supreme Court justices, 14 out of 19 Attorneys General, 21 out of 33 Speakers of the House of Representatives, and 80 out of 134 foreign ministers had been slaveholders.

Philadelphia was a pivotal junction point on the road to freedom. A city with both an anti-slavery society and a slave auction block, it was divided in its allegiances. In 1786, George Washington wrote in a letter to a friend about runaway slaves in Philadelphia, "which a Society of Quakers in the city formed for such purposes have attempted to liberate." Washington was probably referring to the Pennsylvania Abolition Society.

During the era of the Underground Railroad, Independence Hall, or the Old State House as it was called, became the scene of several nationally known fugitive slave trials. Included among the most dramatic trials were participants in the Christiana slave riot in September 1851. More than 30 African Americans were arrested and jailed in Philadelphia and charged with murdering a Maryland slave owner.

In 1855, Jane Johnson, a slave to a North Carolina slave

owner, walked away from her master and was assisted by members of the Philadelphia Underground Railroad to gain freedom with her children. Her furious master, with the assistance of federal officers, arrested her and one of her helpers. The celebrated trial was held in Independence Hall. Johnson was given her freedom. Numerous other escapees were imprisoned and tried inside Independence Hall.

General Lafayette and his African American shown here holding the general's horse during the Revolutionary War at Yorktown, Virginia. It was Lafayette who named "Old State House" Independence Hall.

GENERAL MARQUIS DE LAFAYETTE

The Marquis de Lafayette, French soldier and statesman, spent his long life in the interest of liberty. He fought in both the American and French Revolutions. At age 20, Lafayette became a major general in George Washington's Army. Nicknamed "the boy" by the British, Lafayette praised the valor of African American soldiers and credited his favorite black spy, James Armistead, with helping save his forces from defeat by British General Cornwallis. Lafayette wrote that the black spy "properly acquitted himself with some important communication I gave him and that his intelligence from the enemy's camp were industriously collected an faithfully delivered." Armistead respected Lafayette and changed his name to James Armistead Lafayette in honor of the French general. Lafayette said in a letter, "I would never have drawn my sword in the cause of America if I could have conceived that thereby I was founding a land of slavery."

On another occasion after the Revolutionary War, Lafayette sent a letter to George Washington from France on February 5, 1783, stating: "Now, my dear General, that you are going to enjoy some ease and quiet permit me to propose a plan to you which might become greatly beneficial to the black part of mankind. Let us unite in purchasing a small estate, where we may try the experiment to free Negroes and use them as tenants. Such an example as yours might render it a general practice; and if we succeed in America, I will cheerfully devote a part of my time to render the method fashionable in the West Indies."

Washington replied on April 5, 1783, "The scheme, my dear Marquis, which you proposed as a precedent to encourage the emancipation of the black people in this country from that state of bondage in which they are held is striking evidence of the benevolence of your heart. I shall be happy to join you in so laudable a work but will defer going into a detail of the business till I have the pleasure of seeing you."

The plan never became a reality; however Lafayette and his wife Adrienne did carry out his visionary plan. Between them, they spent thousands of dollars to purchase two plantations in South America, together with 48 slaves for their experiment. Lafayette and his wife forbade sale and whipping of slaves and required the teaching of reading, writing, and arithmetic, and demanded complete freedom as soon as possible.

CHRIST CHURCH

Located on Second Street above Market Street, the Old Christ Church building on the present site began in 1727 and was completed in 1754 with the addition of the tower and spire. George Washington, Thomas Jefferson, Betsy Ross, and seven signers of the Declaration of Independence occupied pews in Old Christ Church. Five signers of the Constitution were buried in Christ Church burial ground. The most noteworthy grave in the yard belongs to Benjamin Franklin. The ubiquitous and creative Franklin composed the following epitaph 40 years before his death:

> "The Body of Benjamin Franklin, Printer
> (Like the cover of an old book, Its contents
> torn out And stript of its lettering and gilding)
> Lies here, food for worms. But the work shall
> not be lost, for it will appear once more. In a
> new and more elegant edition, revised and
> corrected by the author."

Franklin died April 17, 1790.

The records of Christ Church showed that African Americans were baptized and married, and were members of the congregation as early as 1717. There was a minister who had special charge of religious services for them. The baptismal and marriage records of Christ Church still exist. For example free African Americans listed in Christ Church's Baptismal Records, 1717-1760, included:

June 16, 1717	Jane, a free black, aged 40 years and her daughter Jane, aged 3 weeks.
August 13, 1748	Sussee Frame, a free black adult.
August 24, 1748	Rose Watkins, a free black woman
June 22, 1752	Dinah-wife of Richard, a free black and son John
July 26, 1752	Ambo-adult female
July 26, 1752	Amy-adult female and her infant son Anthony
November, 1753	Sarah-mulatto-adult female
November, 1755	Emanuel Woodbe and his wife and their daughters Mary Ann and Dianna
March 3, 1756	Hester, daughter of John and Margaret Lincoln, free blacks
June, 1757	Phillis, daughter of William and Mary Derrom, free blacks
June, 1757	Sarah, daughter of John and Tenah Moore, free blacks

June, 1758	Mintis Ginnings, male adult
February, 1759	John, son of John and Tenah Moore (above)
March, 1759	Mary Lambert, adult female
April, 1760	Rachel, infant daughter of Coffee and Letitia Commings, free blacks

As this list makes clear, parishioners were not always baptized right after birth, as is the custom today.

MARRIAGE RECORDS AT CHRIST CHURCH

September 27, 1728	Francis and Violetta Bone were married
March 3, 1745	Jacob Simons and Tinea Smith, free blacks
December 27, 1745	Titus and Ruth, slaves of George Emlyn
October 1, 1748	Quako and Hannah, slaves of Mr. Allen Sturgeon
August 10, 1755	Archibald Hector and Violet
June 1, 1757	John Moore, a free black and Philis Arthur

October 2, 1757	William Keen and Cornelia Ray, a free black
March 15, 1766	Thomas Augustus and Beneta – black slaves
June 21, 1766	Jack, black slave of Downe York, and Mary
March 21, 1767	Richmond, black slave of Mrs. Dunlap and Sarah, slave of Mr. Harris
September 30, 1767	Audjo, black slave of Margt. McLaughlin and Rose A. Mason's slave
December 31, 1767	Polydore, black slave of Mrs. Allabz and Phyllis, a slave of Mrs. McMurtrie
July 25, 1768	John Fry and Margaret Swelley, free blacks
March 1, 1769	Caesar and Phillis, blacks belonging to Capt. Jenkins
May 1, 1769	Richard Croomes and Hagar Johnson, black slaves of free black Joseph Graisbury

Benjamin Franklin's wife, Deborah, regularly attended Christ Church. On one occasion, she went to hear 17 African American children catechized. She was so impressed with the behavior of the children that she decided to send her young enslaved boy Othello, whom she and her husband purchased in 1757. She also permitted two slaves to attend Christ Church School that operated Wednesdays and Fridays for religious instruction for African American youth.

THREE

BEN FRANKLIN, ALICE OF DUNK'S FERRY, THE PRESIDENT'S HOUSE AND THE LIBERTY BELL

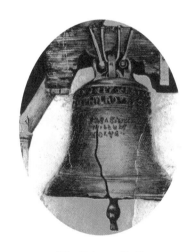

The Liberty Bell

he imposing Franklin Square, named for Benjamin Franklin, occupies a large tract of land between Race and Vine Streets on Sixth Street. It is one of several sites honoring the memory of Franklin in the Philadelphia area. On the subject of people of African descent, Franklin's attitude was at first ambivalent.

Though he published Quaker abolitionist Benjamin Lay's controversial 271-page book entitled *All Slave Keepers that Keep the Innocent in Bondage, Apostates Pretending to Lay Claim to the Pure and Holy Christian Religion*, Franklin and his wife Deborah probably purchased Peter and Jemima in the decade between 1730 and 1740. In a letter written to his mother who lived in Boston in 1750, he stated, "We conclude to sell them both the first good opportunity; for we do not like Negro servants." The letter is documented in Donald W. Labaree's *The Papers of Benjamin Franklin*. His remark did not represent any racial prejudice against African peoples; he was not pleased with their work habits. Despite Franklin's increasing distaste for owning the enslaved couple, Franklin and his wife did not sell Peter and Jemima.

In later years, Franklin purchased another slave named Othello to assist his wife as a house servant, replacing Peter, who Franklin had taken to London. Othello died in 1760. In 1764, in a pamphlet entitled *What is Sauce for the Goose is also Sauce for the Gander*, Franklin's political opponents openly accused him of keeping a black paramour named Barbara, whom some of Franklin's contemporaries called an illicit intimate or prostitute. He was also accused openly in another pamphlet called *A Humble Attempt at Scurrility*, published in 1765. Franklin seems to have made no attempt to deny it.

Shortly before the American Revolution, under the influence of three anti-slavery leaders, Anthony Benezet and Thomas Paine of Philadelphia and Granville Sharp of England, Franklin's attitude towards slavery changed permanently. He was elected to the Pennsylvania Abolition Society in 1787 and later served as the society's president.

Franklin was a member of the convention that formed the Constitution of the United States in 1787. In 1789, he sent a petition to Congress that he signed as president of the Pennsylvania Abolition Society, asking them to exert the full extent of the power vested in them by the Constitution in discouraging the traffic of human species.

BLACK ALICE OF DUNK'S FERRY

Although little is known of this fascinating woman, Black Alice is included on these pages because she lived so long that she became an oral historian, a memory source for those whose lives shared the same time span.

She was so well respected that she was included with such others as Joan of Arc and Empress Catherine I of Russia in a book of biographical sketches, *Eccentric Biography; or Memoirs of Remarkable Female Characters, Ancient and Modern*, published in 1803 by Isaiah Thomas.

In 1686, Alice was born in Philadelphia of enslaved parents who had been brought from Barbados. She lived in Philadelphia until the age of 10. A slave owner then moved her to Dunk's Ferry, 17 miles up the Delaware River in Bucks County.

This remarkable woman vividly recalled William Penn, the "propri-

Black Alice used to light William Penn's pipe and collected tolls at a Delaware River bridge

etor" of Pennsylvania. Whenever he stopped in her area to refresh himself with a pipe, she often lit it.

Alice remembered the ground on which Philadelphia stands when it was a wilderness, when Native Americans hunted wild game in the woods, while panthers, wolves, and other beasts of the forest prowled about the wigwams and cabins in which the Indians lived. She lived as a slave in the Dunk's Ferry vicinity until the end of her life, collecting tolls at the bridge for some 40 years.

She vividly recalled the original wooden structure of her beloved church, Christ Church in Philadelphia. The ceiling of it could be touched with her hands. The bell to call the people to worship was hung in the crotch of a nearby tree. She was remembered as galloping on horseback to Christ Church at age 95. Alice gradually lost her sight between the ages of 96 and 100. Miraculously, it returned. While blind, she was still skillful at catching fish and would row herself out into the stream to do so. She seldom returned without a handsome supply of fish for her owner's table. He hair was perfectly white when she died.

Alice survived the first president of the United States, George Washington, and died at the age of 116 in Bristol, Pennsylvania.

WASHINGTON SQUARE

Located between Sixth and Seventh Streets and Walnut and Locust Streets, Washington Square was one of William Penn's five squares. It originally was called Southeast Square during the colonial period, and later was known as Congo Square. While enslaved Africans generally were compelled to learn their owners' language to understand their commands and to communicate with other enslaved Africans, they consistently refused to abandon their linguistic connection with their homeland. They were remarkably successful in retaining elements of their native language. This was typical of many defiant and proud Africans, both freed and enslaved.

The name "Congo" referred to that part of Africa now called Zaire. During colonial Philadelphia, enslaved Africans were brought to Congo Square once a month before they were sold and transported to other counties in Pennsylvania and elsewhere.

Similar to the enslaved Africans who gathered at Congo Square in New Orleans, Louisiana, these enslaved Africans danced, sang, cooked traditional foods, and conversed in various languages with free Africans in what is known today as the Black Grapevine, naming objects, places, and events unfamiliar to whites.

Musical instruments were also seen in the square and were similar to those used in West Africa and the Congo. Both freed

A group of African people from the West Indies dancing in "Congo Square," Washington Square in Philadelphia.

and enslaved Africans had some knowledge of banjos, fiddles, violins, and instruments made from bones, especially drums. A number of traditional African dances were performed in the square comparable to those performed in Congo Square in New Orleans, Charleston, South Carolina, and New York City. These dances embraced leaps, hops, skips, jumps, falls, and turns of all descriptions. They included dances called the Bamboula, the Ring Shout, or Circle Dance, the Juba and many others that used a variety of body movements.

In 2002, the National Park Service Independence National Historical Park staff provided the square the following interpretation: "Only free and enslaved African Americans brought a measure of mirth to this Square which according to oral tradition, they called 'Congo Square.'"

One 19th century historian wrote that during fairs and holidays perhaps as many as a thousand black Philadelphians came here to dance "after the manner of their several nations in Africa, speaking and singing in their native dialects...over the sleeping dusk below." He also wrote of those from Guinea (a term once used to encompass people of several African areas) "going to the graves of their friends early in the morning and there leaving them victuals and rum." They also offered libations to their ancestors.

PHILADELPHIA'S PRESIDENT'S HOUSE
WHERE SLAVES WERE HELD IN BONDAGE

In 2002, Edward Lawler, a Philadelphia architectural enthusiast, discovered the remains of President George Washington's former residence and his slave quarters revealed while archaeologists working for the National Park Service were excavating the future site for the Liberty Bell's new $12.6 million glass-enclosed pavilion at Sixth and Market Streets, Philadelphia.

Wealthy Quaker Robert Morris permitted Washington to use the mansion and property that became the nation's first presidential residence. Washington kept eight slaves in quarters when Philadelphia was the national capital from 1790 to 1800. When President Washington occupied the mansion with his household staff of 30, including the eight slaves, he did extensive rebuilding, adding servant and slave quarters just beyond the threshold of the new Liberty Bell pavilion.

Prior to President Washington's move, General Benedict Arnold, the once trusted patriot who later turned traitor, lived there. During the British occupation of Philadelphia, General Sir William Howe, commander of the British Army during the Revolution, made the mansion his headquarters.

The President's House and the site of the new Liberty Bell pavilion became a subject of controversy when the public was informed that the former executive mansion, slave quarters, and stable lay underneath or within a few yards of the new pavilion. At first, National Park Service officials contended the story of Washington's slaves was separate from that of the Liberty Bell and that this slave story is best told in another place, not at the pavilion built atop Washington's slave quarters. Upon receiving intense publicity and criticism in the media, the National Park Service agreed to build the new Liberty Bell Pavilion as planned, but also to find a dignified means to commemorate the institution of slavery in its exhibits.

Washington violated the law of the Commonwealth when he brought his slaves to Philadelphia. The Pennsylvania Abolition Society members did not confront the President to inform him that he was violating the Pennsylvania Gradual Act of 1780 that outlawed slavery. Before Washington became President, he was aware of the law. On April 12, 1786, he wrote a letter to Robert Morris, the former treasurer of the Continental Congress. In his letter, Washington pleaded on behalf of slaveholders whose assets for litigation could not match those of the Pennsylvania Abolition Society.

"When slaves who are happy and contented with their present masters are tampered with and seduced to leave them, and when practice of this kind falls on a man, whose purse will not measure that of the Society, and he loses his property for want of means to defend it; it is oppression… and not humanity… because it introduces more evil than one can cure."

Long after the United States capital had moved to Washington D.C. in 1830, Philadelphia merchant Nathaniel Burt had the President's house demolished. However, the entire eastern wall of the house, a portion of the western wall, and part of the foundation survived. On July 3, 2002, on the eve of Independence Day, a group of nearly 500 predominantly African American citizens calling themselves the Avenging the Ancestors Coalition gathered at the old site and at the present site of the Liberty Bell pavilion, demanding erection of a memorial honoring enslaved African American ancestors. They performed a religious ceremony offering libations in honor of Washington's slaves held unlawfully in bondage — Hercules, Richmond, Austin, Moll, Giles, Paris, Christopher Sheels, and Oney Judge. Hercules, the chief cook at Mt. Vernon and the President's House in Philadelphia, was known for his exceptional culinary skills. It was reported that he earned money each year selling leftovers from Washington's kitchen.

Hercules, nicknamed "Uncle Harkless" by the children, was married to a dour slave woman named Lame Alice, a seamstress, and they had three children. However, Alice died in 1787, leaving her husband to raise their children alone. When Hercules learned he was being transferred to Philadelphia in 1790, he asked that his son Richmond accompany him. Richmond was a kitchen worker at the president's house.

Besides being an exceptional cook, Hercules was known for his boisterous, flamboyant, and proud personality. He was chief chef when Washington used the Dreshler-Morris house as his residence in 1794. Washington had promised Hercules that he would never sell him. Being dissatisfied with his enslaved conditions in Philadelphia, he later escaped, eventually going to New York City in March 1797, the day that Washington returned to Mt. Vernon. Hercules' six-year-old daughter spoke mighty words a month after her father ran away. When Prince Louis Philippe of France visited Mt. Vernon, his manservant spoke with Hercules' daughter, and ventured that she must have been sad that she would never see her father again. The young child reportedly replied, "Oh sir! I am very glad because he free now!"

The celebrated American artist Gilbert Stuart is reported to have painted a portrait of Hercules, Washington's "high accomplished" cook. Richmond, Hercules' son, worked as a scullion in the President's House kitchen and swept chimneys for his first year in Philadelphia. He later attempted to escape like his father. Richmond was taken back to Mt. Vernon and his fate is unknown. Moll, a middle-aged dour slave woman was maid to Martha Washington and probably served as a nanny for her grandchildren. She was reported to have been standing in the door of Washington's bedroom when he died on December 14, 1799.

Giles, a male slave, worked as a footman and driver. In Philadelphia, he lived in the slave quarters next to the President House stables. Paris, a teenager, also lived in the slave quarters next to the stables. In 1791, he accompanied Washington on his southern tour and drove the baggage wagon. Austin, the half brother of Oney Judge, worked as a waiter and footman in Mt. Vernon. Austin was trusted to make long trips on his own. He married a slave woman named Charlotte and they had five children.

Christopher Sheels and Paris performed various jobs while employed in the Philadelphia White House. Sheels, age 15, a nephew of William (Billy Lee), Washington's favorite slave, was body servant to the President. Christopher is believed to have known how to write. Washington reportedly discovered a note outlining Christopher's plot to escape from Mount Vernon and foiled it.

Oney Judge, the daughter of an enslaved woman named Betty and a white indentured servant, Andrew Judge, a native of England, performed tasks such as churning butter, spinning thread, making soap, laundry, cooking, and weaving. She was 15 years old when Washington brought her to Philadelphia as the personal servant of Martha.

Desiring to be free, Oney Judge, like Hercules, gained her freedom by "self-liberation" in 1796. She escaped from Philadelphia by ship to Portsmouth, New Hampshire. After she escaped to New Hampshire, Judge attempted to negotiate with Washington before his death for her freedom, but he refused her plea. When he learned of Oney's whereabouts, the President asked the Secretary of the Treasury for help to recover her, explaining that "the ingratitude of the girl, who was brought up and treated more like a child than a servant...ought not to escape impunity." A plan to seize her and put her on a ship to Virginia was thwarted by members of the Portsmouth, New Hampshire, community, who warned Oney and sheltered her from capture.

She settled with a free African American family, found work as a seamstress, and eventually married a man named Jack Staines and bore three children. George Washington attempted to have her kidnapped from New Hampshire and returned to him many years after her escape. Oney never felt that her freedom was secure until Washington's death.

Years later, when she guessed her age to be more than 80, Oney Judge Staines agreed to be interviewed about her life. She had escaped because she did not want to be a slave, and she supposed at the time of her decision that if she returned to Virginia, she would never have another chance to escape. At Portsmouth, she learned to read and was converted to Christianity. She said that even though she had known a hard life in poverty, she held no regrets because she had her freedom.

Troublesome slaves, who frequently ran away seeking self-liberation, when apprehended by slave hunters or local officials, were sometime branded on their forehead, cheeks of their face or on their chest with red, hot branding irons.

Much of this historical documentation is recorded from historians Anne Coxe Toogood and Mary V. Thompson, who documented information on the President's House and Washington's slaves for many years.

Other African Americans, both enslaved and free, had been intermittently connected with the President as they traveled from Mt. Vernon to Philadelphia. For example, William (Billy) Lee, Washington's favorite slave, was present at the President's House. Lee probably married Margaret Thomas, a free African American woman in the "City of Brotherly Love."

Count Francisco Arese in his book *A Trip to the Prairies* (1834) recalls being present at a Fourth of July banquet in Virginia with 160 white men. One of the guests of honor was a Negro who had served with George Washington 50 years before. "He had gone everywhere with the brave general and for that reason half a century later he was allowed the honor once a year of sitting down to a table with white men."

This African American guest was probably William (Billy) Lee, George Washington's trusted former slave and friend who was given his freedom. Leaving Lee a pension, Washington's will stated it was given "as a testimony of my sense of his attachment to me and for his faithful services during the Revolutionary War."

Samuel Fraunces, another free person of African descent whom some writers incorrectly identify as white, came to Philadelphia at General Washington's request to serve as steward of the President's House, and was placed in charge of both indentured servants and enslaved African Americans.

JOURNAL OF CONGRESS.

MONDAY, April 4, 1785.

Congreſs aſſembled—Preſent as before,

On the report of a committee conſiſting of Mr. King, Mr. R. R. Livingſton and Mr. Ellery, to whom was referred a memorial of Samuel Frauncis.

Reſolved. That the ſecretary of Congreſs take a leaſe from Samuel Frauncis for his houſe, now occupied by the public, for the term of two years, at the rate of eight hundred and twelve dollars, and one half of a dollar a year.

That a warrant be drawn in favor of the ſaid Samuel Frauncis, for the ſum of ſixteen hundred and twenty-five dollars, on account of the ſaid rent, and to diſcharge a mortgage on ſaid houſe.

That in conſideration of the ſingular ſervices of the ſaid Samuel Frauncis, and of his advances to the American priſoners, the ſum of two thouſand dollars be paid to the ſaid Samuel Frauncis, on account of the loan office certificates in his hands, and that they be delivered up and cancelled.

TUESDAY, April 5, 1785.

Congreſs aſſembled—Preſent as before.

Congreſs.

Samuel Fraunces, born in the West Indies, owned Fraunces Tavern in New York City, where General Washington and his officers often dined. Research reveals that Fraunces was listed as white in the 1790 census of Heads of Families in New York City and Country. The census takers mistakenly identified him as white because of his fair skin. The designation is not surprising for many mulattos conveniently used their Caucasian appenrance to cross racial barriers. Moreover, unless their racial identity was known, they were presumed white from appearance. Fraunces was called "Black Sam" and his daughter, Phoebe, was described as being "shy and dark".

President John Adams, second President of the United States, also lived in the house with his equally famous wife Abigail. The Adams were adamant anti-slavery advocates. Adams once said, "Negro slavery is an evil of colossal magnitude."

John and Abigail's son, himself a president, John Quincy Adams, also thought that slavery was an evil institution. Adams had an opportunity to do something about it in 1841 as congressmen. He sought and won freedom for the slaves involved in the

Amistad case before the United States Supreme Court. The *Amistad* case has been acclaimed by historians as the most celebrated slave mutiny of the 19th century. In 1839, a group of slaves abroad the *Amistad*, a Spanish slave ship on the way to Cuba, freed themselves under the leadership of Joseph Cinque and killed all but two of the crew. After the ship was steered to New England, the slaves were captured and charge with piracy and murder.

WAGE, INDENTURED, AND SLAVE LABOR

Washington depended on as many as 25 servants to run his household. He employed a variety of help typically available in his day, blending free, indentured, and slave labor to accomplish the day-to-day household business. He hired mostly free white ser-

Joseph Cinque, hero of the Amistad. In 1839, slaves who were captured in Africa as the Amistad was sailing toward Cuba freed themselves under the forceful leadership of Cinque and took over the Spanish ship. Upon landing in New England, with charges of mutiny against them, former President John Quincy Adams represented the Africans before the United States Supreme Court and won the case. The Africans were given their freedom. The Amistad case attracted international attention.

vants. These salaried workers ranged from the President's secretaries, the steward, and the housekeeper at the top to the low-ranking stable hands, scullions, waiters, and maids at the bottom.

President Washington also purchased indentured servants. These European immigrants agreed to work a set time in exchange for their passage to America. Indentured servants were not free until they had completed the terms of their contract. Washington visited the docks of Philadelphia to pay for the indentures of two young Dutch servants who joined the large household at this site.

President Washington's household also included as many as eight African American slaves from Mount Vernon, his Virginia plantation. As the opportunity arose, he replaced them with some local hired hands.

Enslaved Africans working on a colonial American seaport.

PHILADELPHIA AS A CENTER FOR THE ABOLITION MOVEMENT

President Washington was sensitive to the fact that Philadelphia harbored a growing free African population — 2,000 in 1790 — and an influential body of abolitionists who helped pass the first Gradual Emancipation Act (1780) in the new nation. While it freed no slaves immediately, the act raised expectations and promises for a brighter future. The law specified that slaves brought into Pennsylvania from outside the state were entitled to their freedom after six months. Initially, President Washington observed this provision by sending his slaves out of state before the six-month deadline. Pennsylvania's legislature subsequently exempted federal government employees and Congress from the six-month law during their service in Philadelphia.

Even with this change in the law, Washington recognized the danger of bringing his slaves to Philadelphia. He already had admitted his mixed feelings towards slavery and abolitionism by writing, "No man living wishes more sincerely than I do to see the abolition" of slavery, but "when slaves who are happy & content to remain with their present masters are tampered with & seduced to leave them…it introduces more evils than it can cure."

In 1781, Lord Cornwallis' army captured 15 of George Washington's Mount Vernon slaves and placed them on British vessels. Five of these slaves who were taken to Philadelphia were recovered after the war.

In Philadelphia, abolitionists had made notable progress. The city's tradition of Quaker values and religious toleration spawned a diverse population of more than 40,000 people, many of whom sympathized with the active abolitionists. The emerging free African American community also was uniting under strong leadership. Together they created a climate that made Philadelphia a risky place to keep slaves.

Washington was unanimously elected the first president of the United States. He had led the army that fought for the Revolution's ideal that all men are "created equal" and have the right to "life, liberty and the pursuit of happiness." And yet, he owned more than 300 plantation slaves. Washington grappled with this contradiction during his later life.

In the year of his death he lamented that he had too many slaves. "To sell the overplus I cannot, because I am principled against this kind of traffic in human species. To hire them out is almost as bad, because they could not be disposed of in families to any advantage, and to disperse families I have an aversion. What then is to be done?"

By his will of July 9, 1799, he freed all those people he personally owned. (Martha's estate legally owned most of the Mount Vernon slaves.) He also left instructions for his family to provide lifetime support for the old or disabled among them, as well as to care for orphaned children to the age of 25.

THE LIBERTY BELL AND THE FRIENDS OF FREEDOM

On Independence Mall, where American liberty was claimed and proclaimed, there stands the historic symbol so reverently preserved as the noblest utterance of human rights in a charter of freedom. In fact, a slave holder, Isaac Norris, Jr., commissioned it. In 1751, Norris was speaker of the Pennsylvania Assembly and proposed the installation of this bell in the newly-erected steeple of the old Philadelphia State House (now Independence Hall) in commemoration of the 50th anniversary of William Penn's Charter of Privilege. The Liberty Bell was cast many years before sentiment for an independent America developed.

First hung in 1753, this bell bore the inscription, "Proclaim Liberty throughout the Land unto all the Inhabitants thereof." Exactly how this bell got its familiar name is unknown. Noted abolitionists such as Francis D. Pastorious, John Woolman, George Bryan, Benjamin Lay, George Keith, Anthony Benezet and George Sandiford were all dead when a fiery, anti-slavery group known as the Friends of Freedom were the first to popularize the symbol of the bell. This group of abolitionist and literary figures that called for immediate liberation for all enslaved persons toiling in bondage and continued promotion of security protection and improvement of Free African Americans was founded in Boston in 1839. The group issued a famous series of publications entitled *The Liberty Bell.* They included nationally known personalities such as William Lloyd Garrison, John Greenleaf Whitter, Lucretia Mott, Harriet Beecher Stowe, Elizabeth Barrett Browning, Lydia Maria Child, William Wells Brown, and Henry David Thoreau.

Frederick Douglass contributed one of his earliest writings to the publication. Douglass, a former escaped slave, later became a skilled anti-slavery speaker, praised for his wit, argument, sarcasm, and pathos. Douglass' friends included fiery abolitionist John Brown and Underground Railroad

Harriet Beecher Stowe, the author of the international best seller Uncle Tom's Cabin *was born into an abolitionist family. Stowe sold 300,000 copies of her book during the first year of publication in 1852. The book's circulation was forbidden in the South.*

conductor Harriet Tubman, and he was an advisor to President Abraham Lincoln.

Douglass came to Independence Hall in 1844 to speak out against slavery while he was legally a runaway slave from Maryland. He was in his twenties and risked being apprehended and returned to enslavement. Most African Americans and some white abolitionists did not honor the Independence Day celebration on the Fourth of July. They celebrated instead British West Indies Emancipation, when slavery was abolished on August 1, 1834. In Rochester, New York, where he was living at that time in 1852, Douglass delivered his famous "Fifth of July" speech. He agreed to speak, but not on the day of the Fourth of July celebration.

"This Fourth of July" Douglass reminded his audience, "is yours, not mine; you rejoice, I must mourn. To drag a man in fetters into the grand illuminated temple of liberty and call upon him to join you in joyous anthem were inhuman mockery and sacrilegious irony. Do you mean, citizens, to mock me, by asking me to speak today?" Many scholars consider Douglass' speech one of the greatest orations in American history.

Many African Americans in the nation maintained a feeling of reservation toward celebrating on July 4th, because of the danger of assault by boisterous, anti-black white people who had drunk too much. When, in 1859, the Banneker Institute decided to celebrate the Fourth of July, the Anglo-African newspaper published in Boston remarked that such an observance was something new in Philadelphia and at variance with the general practice among African Americans coast to coast.

That same year, 1859, John Brown was hanged for his ill-fated raid on Harper's Ferry, West Virginia. Brown had many abolitionist friends in Philadelphia. Hundreds of supporters and southern sympathizers lined Broad Street to view his coffin as it passed through the city. Mayor Alexander Henry ordered that

John Brown, son of an Underground Railroad station master. He was connected with the Underground Railroad wherever he traveled. Brown brooded about the evils of slavery, becoming increasingly obsessed with the idea that God chose him to liberate slaves by force. Finally, he plotted his ill-fated raid on the U.S. Arsenal at Harper's Ferry. Federal troops led by Col. Robert E. Lee subdued the insurrection. Brown and his followers were hanged in December 1859, having helped set the nation on the road to the Civil War. Shown here is "John Brown's Last Moment" by artist Thomas Hovenden.

Brown's body be moved through Philadelphia without pause and assembled a large police detachment to keep order.

Nationally known Quaker John Greenleaf Whittier, the Poet Laureate of New England and contributor to the pamphlet the *Liberty Bell*, by the Friends of Freedom, while living in Philadelphia edited the *Pennsylvania Freeman*, an anti-slavery newspaper. He first came to the city in 1833, as a delegate from Massachusetts to organize the American Anti-Slavery Society. The convention of fewer than 75 people met at the Adelphi house on Fifth Street below Walnut and, along with William Lloyd Garrison and the Reverend Samuel May, drafted the now famous

Declaration of Anti-Slavery Sentiments. The document was written principally at night in the attic of the home of prominent African American abolitionist Dr. James C. McCrummell.

The Declaration of Anti-Slavery Sentiments was read on The Fourth of July in many African American communities. Years later during his retirement Whittier stated, "I set a higher value on my name as appended on the Anti Slavery Declaration in 1833, than on the title page of any book." His Quaker coat had been pelted with eggs and the newspaper office of the *Pennsylvania Freeman* burned over his head by a rowdy Philadelphia anti-abolitionist crowd.

The location surrounding the Liberty Bell is considered one of the nation's most significant African American sites. In 2001, archaeological excavation uncovered the former home of James Oronoke Dexter, one of Philadelphia's African American founding fathers. A close associate of Richard Allen and Absalom Jones, he was a prominent member of the Free African Society. His wooden house was located on Fifth Street just north of Cherry Street.

A coachman by trade, Dexter used his home as a meeting place for the founding of St. Thomas African Episcopal Church. He was in charge of providing bricks and stone to erect the church. Included in this integrated neighborhood were both freed and enslaved African people who worked for wealthy, white families in the area.

The site became a subject of controversy when it was discovered that Independence Hall National Park officials planned to build a 12-station bus depot there for the national park.

FOUR

STEPHEN GIRARD –
AMERICA'S WEALTHY MIDAS
AND THE YELLOW FEVER 1793.

Stephen Girard, wealthiest American during his time, slave owner, and shipping merchant. Accused of keeping Toussaint L'Ouverture's vast wealth. He stipulated in his will that Girard College admit poor, white boys only.

tephen Girard, one of the richest Americans of his time, was born in Bordeaux, France, in 1750. His father, Pierre, a wealthy merchant and slave trader, settled with his family in St. Dominique (now Haiti) in the West Indies. Girard became a sea captain when he was 23 years old. In 1776, he settled in Philadelphia and established vast financial holdings.

Girard married Mary Lum, an attractive 18-year-old orphan and the daughter of a penniless ship worker in the Northern Liberties section of Philadelphia. Their marriage was not successful largely due to Mary's inability to produce children. According to several biographies written on Girard's life, his wife was admitted a lunatic "paying patient" on August 25, 1790, after wandering through Philadelphia streets and moving through a succession of boarding houses. Girard had recoiled against committing her, but became convinced her irrationality might bring her harm. Five months after Mary was admitted to an insane asylum, she became pregnant and rumors began to circulate that a black sailor had gotten into the loosely guarded cells.

The insane asylum officials asked Girard to remove her, afraid Girard might insist on including his wife's maternity and childcare in the original fees. But Girard permitted his wife to remain in the asylum. On March 3, 1791, an infant was born. "The child was put out to nurse with John Hatcher's wife at $10 per week." However, the child died in August.

During the great Yellow Fever Plague of 1793, Girard provided both advice and money to city officials who were combating the terrifying pestilence.

Girard's brother John and his attractive black mistress Hannah had a daughter named Rosetta in 1772 in St. Dominique. Girard himself owned two other slaves, including Abraham, a 12-year-old boy whom he bought in Virginia in 1778. Abraham proved to be troublesome; he ran away yearly. On one occasion, Girard placed an advertisement in a Philadelphia newspaper offering a reward for Abraham that read:

> a likely Negro-six feet high, had on when he went away a round black woolen hat, a dark brown coatee, with white buttons, reyers duck trousers, white thread stockings and shoes with plated buckles.

Another one of Girard's slaves, Sam, a few years younger than Abraham, according to Girard's brother John "slipped away to revel in forbidden pleasures." John wanted his brother to brand the boy because he was a chronic deserter, but Girard did not carry out his brother's demand.

Girard was known as a man who imposed heavy workloads on all his employees and had no patience with any one, slave or free, who shirked their duties.

Girard was the chief financial adviser to the United States government during the War of 1812. After Congress failed to renew the charter of the first bank of the United States in 1811, Girard bought most of the stock and buildings of the Bank, and made the Bank of Stephen Girard one of the soundest firms in the country.

Girard later helped the government finance the War of 1812. In 1816, he bought $3 million worth of stock in the Second Bank of the United States and became one of its directors. There appears to be some confusion and controversy on Stephen Girard, his wealth, and how he came about the large accumulation.

Several writers and historians, including Joel A. Rogers in *One Hundred Amazing Facts about the Negro*, report that Toussaint L' Ouverture, the Haitian liberator, saved six million gold francs, equivalent to that sum in dollars today. After the treacherous capture of Toussaint by the French, led by Napoleon's brother-in-law on the island of St. Dominique, Girard would not turn over this money to Toussaint's family. During his nine-month imprisonment in the French Alps where Toussaint was held, he was excessively harassed by Napoleon's agents to reveal where the money was hidden. L'Ouverture died in his cold dungeon without revealing the source of the money concealment. L'Ouverture planned to make Dahomey (now Benin) in West Africa his base for fighting the slave trade.

Another view of Girard's wealth pertains to a legal suit entered in Common Pleas Court in Philadelphia in 1886 by counsel for Madame Rose de Laulanie, of Paris, the sole surviving descendant of L'Ouverture. According to her claim, Toussaint, when ordered by Napoleon to Paris, feared arrest and handed over his fortune, two million francs, to Stephen Girard, who was in St. Dominique, under the agreement that if Toussaint was detained in Paris, the money was to be used to effect his escape. Girard, Toussaint's descendant said, sailed to Philadelphia and kept the money, however.

Toussaint's descendant could not produce any records or other documents to prove her claim except for oral family tradition. The suit failed. Attorneys representing Girard's estate stated that Girard never had any contacts with L'Ouverture, nor was he present at the time when L'Ouverture, Dessaline, and Christophe led the Haitian Revolt. However, French writer Gragnon-LaCoste in his *Life of Toussaint L'Ouverture*, names the sum as six million francs, and says Girard was in Haiti and never returned the millions entrusted to his care following the events that deprived Toussaint of his liberty.

This author tells also of the litigation that followed in the courts for the money left by Girard to the City of Philadelphia. Other writers speculate that Girard sent one of his agents to Haiti to represent him and to receive the money. Although significant evidence was not presented during the court trial, it is sufficiently persuasive to cry for further investigation by modern attorneys.

Girard owned 30 slaves in New Orleans. He died in 1831; his controversial will set aside a large portion of money to buy coal for poor, white Philadelphians. However, the first person actually

General Toussaint L'Ouverture was considered one of the world's most important military geniuses. A former slave, L'Ouverture along with two other former slaves who became Generals, Jean Jacque Dessaline and Henri Christophe defeated Napoleon forces on the former French Island Saint Dominique (now Haiti). Some historians called L'Ouverture the "Black Napoleon," and called him a military strategic genius.

mentioned in the will was Hannah, Girard's housekeeper and his brother John's black mistress. Girard provided money for her until she died. Girard bequeathed a large sum of money toward establishment of Girard College. A stipulation in his will stated that the college was for "poor, white orphan boys only" and that a high wall should be built around it. The will sparked one of the longest cases in Philadelphia's legal history. Even though the school is situated in the midst of Philadelphia's African American community, the city

Henri Christophe, a 12-year-old boy soldier fighting for American Independence at the Battle of Savannah, Georgia, with a company of black Haitian soldiers sent to America, long before leading the revolution against the French in Haiti. As king of Haiti, he prevented Napoleon from making his sister Pauline Queen of Haiti during Napoleon's ill-fated expedition to that country. During his reign as king, Christophe built his palace and the Citadel, a great fortress that is still standing today. It is considered one of the wonders of the modern world.

adhered to the stipulations for 100 years, until noted African American lawyers Raymond Pace Alexander and Cecil B. Moore challenged it.

Raymond Pace Alexander was the first African American to serve on the Philadelphia Common Pleas Court. He charged the City with discrimination at Girard College in the 1930s. The case was not won until the mid-1960s when Moore, another African American attorney, along with internationally known civil rights leader the Rev. Martin Luther King and hundreds of others joined a protest march to the site of the college. The case was won when the United States Supreme Court decided against the legality of Girard's will. Both African American boys and girls attend the school today.

THE YELLOW FEVER PLAGUE OF 1793 – WHEN TIME STOOD STILL

The Yellow Fever Plague of 1793 has been called one of the strangest episodes in American history. As one writer said, it was "Philadelphia's worst time," with more than 5,000 people dying. During that summer of 1793, a foul and fantastic pestilence struck the inhabitants without warning, disregarding races and class, and citizens began dying by the thousands.

Philadelphia was the national capitol then, and President George Washington declared "matters of private concernment which required him to be elsewhere." Government offices closed. One Quaker woman, Susan Dillwyn wrote, "Poor Philadelphia! Lately so full, so gay and busy, now a mournful solitude."

"People were sick in body and heart, astonished and fearful, paralyzed by the mysterious obscenity about them," wrote author J.H. Powell in his book *Bring Out Your Dead*.

Many people in the city were convinced that the influx of

refugees who poured into Philadelphia to escape from the rebellion-wracked island of Haiti and other West Indian islands was responsible for the pestilence. Vessels carried hundred of white refugees and their slaves, even free people of color. Burying the victims of the plague became a challenge. Doctors turned patients away by the dozens, no matter how wealthy or prominent they were.

Dr. Benjamin Rush and other prominent men of medicine originally thought that Philadelphia's free African community of more than 2,500 citizens were immune from the fever. Rush, Mayor Matthew Clarkson, and Stephen Girard asked Richard Allen, Absalom Jones, and William Gray, all leaders of the African American community, to ask their followers to help bury the dead.

Allen was to supervise the burial, Jones was to organize the nursing, and Gray assisted in organizing work in the city's recovery. It was a time when the question of race was unimportant. It was a time when Philadelphia turned to its black citizens for assistance.

From Wilmington, Delaware, a young Englishman wrote to a friend: "We hear that Philadelphia is dying." The story is told of a young African American woman who was offered "great wages" to go to a sick white man and his wife. "I will not go for money, God will see it and maybe he will send on the fever. But if I go and take no money, he may spare my life." On one hot summer night, a candlelight procession moved to Congo Square (now Washington Square) that was Philadelphia's potter field in 1793. It was estimated that there were 1,000 victims of the fever who were buried there.

Later, a number of African Americans became victims of the fever; they proved as susceptible to it as the whites. They were not infected until the fantastic pestilence had raged a full month. There were a number of other physicians assisting Dr. Benjamin Rush during the epidemic. Dr. David de Cohen Nassy, a Jewish

Dr. Benjamin Rush, signer of the Declaration of Independence, prominent physician, member of the Pennsylvania Abolition Society, owned a slave but was a friend of the Rev. Richard Allen and other members of Philadelphia's African American community.

physician whose family owned a large plantation in Surinam, had freed his young slave Matthew and bought him to Philadelphia. Matthew, while assisting Nassy during the fever, became known as "The French Physician Boy." After the fever, he wrote a report, originally in French, that was the first American Jewish medical publication.

Led by Irish publisher Matthew Cary, whites accused African Americans who courageously offered their services during the deadly plague of stealing money from victims. Their cries could be heard throughout the city, "Bring out your dead, Bring out your dead." To rebut the slanderous misrepresentation of the African American community, Richard Allen and Absalom Jones jointly wrote *A Narrative of the Proceedings of the Black People during the Late, Awful Calamity in Philadelphia in 1794.* It is recorded to have been the first public defense written by African Americans in the United States.

FIVE

HISTORIC GERMANTOWN AND THE DEFENDERS OF INDEPENDENCE AMERICA'S FIRST PROTEST AGAINST SLAVERY – 1688

"You have invariably through the most trying times maintained a constant friendship and attention to the cause of our country and its independence and freedom."

George Washington to Samuel Fraunces

ed by Francis Daniel Pastorius and a small group of other German refugees and Quakers, the first protest against slavery in America occurred on April 18, 1688, in the former Thones Kunders house in Germantown. This group of men who had no previous acquaintance with the horrible institution of slavery was amazed to find it existing in William Penn's colony.

Pastorius and three other men met at the Friends meetinghouse in Germantown on April 18, 1688, and placed their signatures on this historic abolitionist document that stated the reasons why they were against slavery and the "traffic in men's bodies." Pastorius sent the protest document to Abington Friends Meeting, which turned it down. It then was sent to Philadelphia Yearly Meeting, where it was dropped as "radical and untimely."

The original document, now partly faded and with parts illegible, can be found in the archive of the Department of Records, Philadelphia Yearly Meeting of the Religious Society of Friends. A Pennsylvania State Historical Marker honors the site today at 5109 Germantown Avenue.

STENTON

Located in Stenton Park on Windrim Avenue near 18th Street is Stenton. Erected on a former plantation that contained more than 500 acres, it is the home of James Logan, an early Quaker settler of historic Germantown and the appointed secretary to William Penn. Logan designed and built Stenton, as the home was called between 1723 and 1730. Stenton was occupied for a time during the Revolutionary War by General George Washington and later by General Sir William Howe, who made the home his headquarters from which to direct the Battle of Germantown.

On the historic home is a plaque honoring Logan's servant, an African-American woman by the name of Dinah. By her quick thought and presence of mind, Dinah saved the mansion from being burned by British soldiers in the winter of 1777. According to family members many years later, two British soldiers prepared to burn the mansion. When they went to the barn to get straw to set the fire, a British officer rode up with sword drawn and asked Dinah if she had seen any deserters. The wise old servant woman promptly replied that, "Two such have just gone to secrete themselves in the barn." The officer rode to the barn and chased the "deserters" away, and Stenton was saved.

The Logan family continued to live in the mansion for six generations until 1900. Now it is maintained by the National Society of Colonial Dames of America in the Commonwealth of Pennsylvania. A plaque was dedicated in honor of the black woman with this inscription: *In memory of Dinah, faithful colored caretaker of Stenton, who by her quick thought and presence of mind, saved the mansion from being burned by the British soldiers in the winter of 1777.* It is believed to be the first memorial to a former slave reared in Philadelphia. Although historians in the past have said that Dinah was an enslaved woman during the Battle of Germantown, Dinah acquired her own freedom by frequently demanding it from the Logans. William and his wife Hannah freed Dinah in the spring of 1776, a year before the Battle of Germantown.

DAVID RITTENHOUSE HOMESTEAD

Benjamin Rittenhouse was one of the original settlers in Germantown and the father of David Rittenhouse, the celebrated astronomer, scientist, clockmaker, writer and revolutionary. Born in Germantown in 1732, Rittenhouse was also state treasurer, second president of the American Philosophical Society, and director of the United States Mint.

David Rittenhouse, born in Germantown, Philadelphia, Pennsylvania, during the post-Revolution era. Rittenhouse was America's leading scientist. He wrote to Secretary of State Thomas Jefferson stating that Benjamin Banneker was "every instance of genius amongst Negroes is worthy of attention." He added, "because their oppressors seem to lay great stress on their mental abilities." A public square in Philadelphia honors Rittenhouse's name.

The Rittenhouse family moved to a large farm in Norriton, Montgomery County, when David was but two years old. Before the Revolutionary War, Rittenhouse surveyed the boundaries of Pennsylvania. He was known for his friendly relationship with African Americans. Listed among them were Benjamin Banneker, a self-taught Maryland freeborn astronomer and scientist who published several important almanacs and made the first wooden striking clock in America. At the age of 59, Banneker sent a copy of his almanac to Thomas Jefferson, then Secretary of State, along with a letter questioning Jefferson's contradictory views on slavery.

Jefferson was sufficiently impressed with Banneker's work that he appointed him as a member of the commission to survey the new District of Columbia. However, it was David Rittenhouse who provided Banneker with the highest recommendation when he wrote that he found Banneker's calculations sufficiently accurate for an almanac, and his total performance "extraordinary."

"Every instance of genius amongst the Negroes is worthy of attention," Rittenhouse went on to say, "because their oppressors seem to lay great stress on their supposed inferior mental abilities."

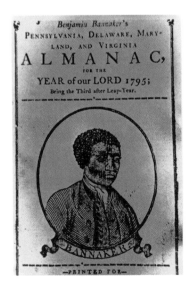

ABOVE: *Benjamin Banneker, born in Maryland of free parents. He was a self-taught mathematician, scientist, and astronomer. He helped to plan the new federal city, Washington, D.C. David Rittenhouse, America's leading scientist, admired Banneker.*

LEFT: *Benjamin Banneker published this almanac for Delaware, Maryland, Pennsylvania, and Virginia in 1795.*

In 1796, when Rittenhouse's funeral oration was delivered, several African Americans were present. Located at 20th Street between Walnut and Locust Street in Philadelphia, is a scenic tree-lined square, one of the original five squares planned by William Penn, now named for David Rittenhouse.

CLIVEDEN – THE HOME OF THE CHIEF JUSTICE OF PENNSYLVANIA AND THE BIRTHPLACE OF RICHARD ALLEN

Located at 6401Germantown Avenue, this large mansion and monument to American history was built by Quaker Benjamin Chew, Chief Justice of Pennsylvania between 1763 and 1767. Cliveden figured most prominently in the Revolutionary War's Battle of Germantown, suffering heavy bombardment by the British. Several soldiers of African descent fought in this historic encounter. Cliveden was also the home of Richard Allen and his family.

Allen was born in 1760 of a "pure African" father and mulatto mother who were slaves. In need of money, Chew sold Allen's family to a Quaker planter named Stokeley near Dover, Delaware. This sale of the entire family in a group was one of the rare exceptions in the complex institution of slavery. Usually individuals were separated and sold because the profits were greater. Allen was converted in 1777 and began his career as a minister three years later. His owner permitted him to conduct prayers and preach in his own house, and was one of Allen's first converts. He made it possible for Allen and his brother to purchase their freedom for $2,000.

Allen preached in Wilmington on September 13, 1783, the first sermon to have been delivered by a person of African descent in that city. In 1786, Allen went to Philadelphia and became a

The Rev. Richard Allen, born a slave in Germantown, Philadelphia, Pennsylvania. Founded Mother Bethel A.M.E. Church. Later became Bishop Founding member of the Free African Society in 1787. Allen was one of the most respected leaders in Philadelphia.

member of the white St. George's Methodist Church, the oldest Methodist Church in the nation. Allen was licensed to preach in 1784 and was permitted to hold services at 5:00 in the morning. Due to the increasing number of African Americans who attended the church to hear Allen preach, tensions increased and white parishioners began to complain.

One Sunday morning, a white sexton met the African American parishioners at the door and sent them to the gallery to sit in "Negro" pews. As Allen observed and heard considerable scuffling he noticed that the trustees were pulling Absalom Jones and William White off their knees. When the prayer was over, the African American parishioners led by Allen and Jones withdrew from the church in a body and St. George Church was "no more plagued with us," wrote Absalom Jones.

The basis for a new fellowship outside St. George was the Free African Society, formed eight months prior to the separation in 1787. This society in reality was a mutual-aid society for the benefit of members who were sick and "widows and fatherless children."

During that period, Allen developed a friendship with Dr. Benjamin Rush, signer of the Declaration of Independence and a slave owner. Allen with two other prominent African Americans, Absalom Jones and James Forten, attended The Willings Alley Free School established for African American children by Anthony Benezet. Adults were permitted to attend the school in the evenings. Assisting Allen with his responsibilities in his church and his community activities was his wife Sarah, whom Allen married in 1810. Soon she embraced other mission work, including assisting slaves on the Underground Railroad. The church itself was a station stop on the freedom network. Allen was also a circuit rider, a preacher who provided religious service to churches in various towns.

Allen founded the African Episcopal Methodist Church (AME) affectionately known as "Mother Bethel" in 1794, at Sixth near Lombard Streets. The original church was an old structure formerly owned by a blacksmith. In 1830 the second church was the site of the first colored political convention in America.

A respected leader and a man with vision, Bishop Richard Allen was an "early advocate" of equal rights for women and gave Jarena Lee, who was born in Cape May, New Jersey, in 1783, an opportunity to preach in his church. An itinerant preacher, Lee traveled throughout the eastern seaboard and preached 178 sermons in one year. She covered 2,325 miles under adverse conditions.

The current building was constructed in 1889 in the same location as three previous structures. Mother Bethel sits on the oldest parcel of land in Philadelphia continually owned by African Americans.

Jarena Lee, born in Cape May, New Jersey, in 1783. Upon arriving in Philadelphia, Lee was encouraged to exercise her talent for speaking by Bishop Richard Allen. When traveling throughout the eastern seacoast, Lee preached 178 sermons, covering 2,325 miles under adverse conditions to deliver her words of inspiration.

THE DESHLER-MORRIS HOUSE (THE GERMANTOWN WHITE HOUSE)

Quaker David Deshler, a merchant and amateur pharmacist, built this historic house facing the cobblestone square at 5442 Germantown Avenue in 1772. While the American Revolution began with the Minutemen at Lexington and Concord in Massachusetts, Germantown also played an important role in the quest for independence. The Deshler-Morris house played a pivotal role in the Battle of Germantown on October 4, 1777.

The conflict ranged from Cliveden in Upper Germantown along the "Great Road," now Germantown Avenue, to Market Square, where the Deshler-Morris house is located. During the Revolutionary War, the very popular British General Sir William Howe occupied Philadelphia in September 1777 and General George Washington's Continental Army retreated to Valley Forge. In early October, a pursuing force of British soldiers reached Germantown. General Howe used the Deshler-Morris House as a headquarters.

The large stone house gets its name from the first and last owners, the latter being Samuel Morris. It is ironic that the house that British General Howe occupied also was used by George Washington when he was President of the United States. Washington leased the house from Colonel Isaac Frank. During the deadly Yellow Fever epidemic in 1793, Washington conducted the affairs of the newly formed republic at the Germantown "White House." Here President Washington presided over meetings with his cabinet—Thomas Jefferson, Alexander Hamilton, Henry Knox, and Edmund Randolph. Hercules, Washington's favorite cook, was at the Deshler house.

Recently, scholars representing the National Park Service of the United States Department of the Interior who administer the Deshler-Morris House have speculated that there could have been other enslaved persons in Washington's Germantown residence.

In 1776, the British, hoping to terminate the war, tried to poison Washington. Their agent, a double-spy, was Thomas Hickey, an Irishman who had won Washington's confidence and had been made his bodyguard. Hickey began winning the heart of the daughter of Samuel Fraunces, Phoebe. Hickey gave the young and attractive woman a dish of poisoned peas to serve

Phoebe Fraunces, daughter of Samuel Fraunces, did even more for her country than her father. She saved the life of General Washington and several of his officers from a plot to poison them. Thomas Hickey, Washington's bodyguard and a spy for the British, poisoned a dish of peas. Phoebe exposed the plot by throwing the peas out the window where some chickens ate the peas and fell dead. Hickey was hanged with a large crowd looking on. Phoebe was described by her contemporaries as being 'shy and dark.'

Washington. Phoebe, despite her love for Hickey, warned Washington, who threw the peas into the yard. Chickens picked them up and fell dead.

Thomas Hickey was hanged before a large crowd in New York City. Had Washington died, America probably would have remained part of the British Empire. Fraunces' racial identification has been documented by several sources. William Hornor, Jr., in his commendably documented article on Fraunces in the *Philadelphia Bulletin*, February 22, 1934, calls him "this fastidious old Negro" and says that he wore a powdered, white wig over his curly hair.

George Washington had mixed emotions about people of African descent. He once sold a young enslaved boy to Barbados to be exchanged for a hogshead of molasses, a cask of rum, and "other good old spirits." But he praised highly Phillis Wheatley's poems when she sent him a copy of her book, published in London in 1773.

One of Wheatley's later poems was dedicated to Washington, a tribute upon his appointment as Commander-in-Chief of the Continental forces (Generalissimo of the Armies of America). Washington sent Wheatley a gracious reply and invited her to visit him whenever she was in the Cambridge, Massachusetts, area. Wheatley was a young enslaved girl who was captured in Senegal, West Africa, at the age of 10, and was owned by a Quaker family in Boston. Her book of poems, entitled *Poems on Various Subjects*, was the first book published by an African American in the United States. Thomas Paine introduced Phillis Wheatley to the Philadelphia public. Benjamin Franklin also praised her works. However, when Thomas Jefferson read her poems, he declared it was beneath his dignity to comment on them.

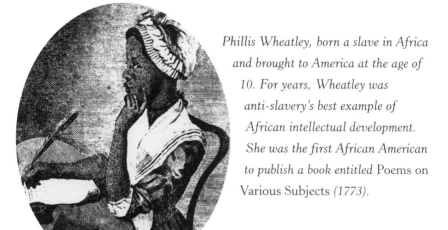

Phillis Wheatley, born a slave in Africa and brought to America at the age of 10. For years, Wheatley was anti-slavery's best example of African intellectual development. She was the first African American to publish a book entitled Poems on Various Subjects *(1773).*

Throughout his life, Washington was the owner of about 300 slaves, including those his wife inherited. When slaves became too difficult to control, he sold them. But Washington did have his "favorite" ones, and history cites certain enslaved persons such as William Lee, bought from Mary Lee in 1768. William Lee accompanied Washington through thick and thin until the Revolutionary War ended and then to the Mount Vernon household with his wife, Margaret Thomas, a free woman from Philadelphia. When Washington died in 1799, his will provided that upon Martha Washington's death, all of his slaves should be liberated, "but to my Mulatto man William (calling himself William Lee) I give immediate freedom." In a famous painting by Edward Savage of Washington's family group, William Lee is in a black suit, white shirt, and dark cravat.

Other enslaved men served as personal attendants to Washington. Among them were Hamet Achmet, skilled as a maker of drums; Primus Hall, who slept beside Washington on a cold winter night; and Christopher Sheels, who personally served Washington during his moments of reflection.

THE JOHNSON HOUSE

Another historic house that is connected to liberty and freedom is located at 6306 Germantown Avenue. This house was built in 1768 by German Quaker Derick Jansen, a tanner by trade who anglicized his name to Johnson. He built the house for his son, John. During the Battle of Germantown on October 4, 1777, bullets and cannonballs left their mark on the door.

During the ante-bellum period, the Johnson House served as a station on the Underground Railroad. Runaway slaves were sheltered in the basement and attic and also were hidden in a smaller building on the property, according to oral tradition.

Speaking in Riddles and Singing in Codes

I have two minds, one mind is for the master to see,
the other mind I know is me.
An old slave saying

Enslaved Africans used various forms of deception and ingenuity to fool their masters and mistresses and overseers, to plan escapes, and to plan revolts. This deception was known within the slave community as "Puttin' on Ole Massa."

When drums were outlawed in many of the colonies because they were used to send coded messages through a communication system known as call and response, African people employed the use of coded spirituals as a form of deception. African American historian Lerone Bennett, Jr. writes:

> Slaves...used music as a medium of communication. The cries and hollers and field calls contained secret messages and code words. In truth, double meaning permeated the whole fabric of this music. One song, for example, used Jesus to mask an open and obvious invitation to the slave to steal away.
> *Steal away, steal away,*
> *Steal away to Jesus,*
> *Steal away, steal away home,*
> *I ain't got long to stay here.*

Self- emancipation carried numerous escapees on their perilous journey to the closest free territory. These coded spirituals conveyed every hidden signal imaginable, songs for escaping, hiding, and expressing danger.

African people who lived in the Sea Islands of South

Carolina and Georgia spoke a language known as Gullah that mixes English words and syntax with those from the Caribbean Islands and especially West Africa to create a speech that is all but incomprehensible to outsiders. This tongue sometimes called Geechee is an important reason why Sea Islanders have preserved a way of life that remains African in some of its essentials.

Because large congregations were discouraged, enslaved and free African people would gather informally and in secret around stone circles, a practice that was used in West Africa. They would speak into the circle in low voices so as not to be heard. Oftentimes both free and enslaved African people marked graves of their family members and other members of their community with unmarked stones and buried them in coffins facing the east.

Hundreds of words derived from West African languages occurred in Gullah, and some have crossbred with English to become common expressions. Here are a few expressions with the languages from which they may have come.

Goober	*Peanut (Kimbundu)*
Gumbo	*Okra (Tsiluba*
Heh	*Yes (Vai)*
Hoodoo	*Bad Luck (Hausa*
Yambi	*Yam (Vai)*
Chigger	*Small Flea (Wolof)*
Nana	*Grandmother (Jwi)*
Biddy	*Small Chicken (Congo)*
Buckra	*White Man (Igbo)*

Even the improvised lyrics of modern Calypso singers in the Caribbean Islands follow the ancient African tradition of singing songs with double meanings. Calypso music as we know it today originated on the island of Trinidad, where various groups of people from all over the world have been traveling since Columbus discovered it in 1498.

AFRICAN AMERICAN DEFENDERS OF INDEPENDENCE

"You have invariably through the most trying times maintained a constant friendship and attention to the cause of our country and its independence and freedom."
George Washington to Samuel Fraunces

People of African descent took part in all the nation's wars. In March 1770, Crispus Attucks, an enslaved runaway, was the first person killed during the confrontation between colonial citizen and garrisoned British soldiers. Six years before the Declaration of Independence, Attucks led a crowd of colonists to Boston's Dock Square to protest the clubbing death of a youth by a British sentry. Fighting broke out, shots were fired, and Attucks was the first to die during what would become known as the Boston Massacre.

Crispus Attucks, a former runaway slave, was the first man to give his life for American independence during the Boston Massacre on March 5, 1770. In doing so he sparked the American Revolution.

Slave Advertisement for Crispus Attucks

The *Boston Gazette and Weekly Journal* of Tuesday, November 20, 1750, advertised the following:

> Ran away from his master William Brown of Framingham, on the 30th of September last, a mulatto fellow, about 27 years of age, named Crispus, well set six feet two inches high, short curled hair, knees nearer together than common. Had on a light-colored buckskin fustian jacket, new buckskin breeches, blue yarn stockings and a checked shirt. Whoever shall take up said runaway and convey him to his above said master at Framingham, shall have Ten Pounds, old tenor, reward and all necessary charges paid.

From the earliest battles, at Lexington and Concord in the spring of 1775, African American patriots including Peter Salem, Barzillai Lewis, and Salem Poor distinguished themselves during the Battle of Bunker Hill (Breed's Hill) on June 17, 1775. Poor was later commended for his valiant performance in this battle. Some 5,000 African Americans, both enslaved and free, participated in Washington's Continental Army. Originally, soldiers of African descent were not welcomed. Some slave owners sent their slaves to war promising them freedom, instead of going themselves. They were attracted to the same ideas of liberty and freedom that white men such as George Washington, Thomas Jefferson, Thomas Paine, Benjamin Franklin, and Patrick Henry wanted.

Articulate African American sailors displayed courage on the seas and shared some of John Paul Jones' celebrated victories.

Peter Salem shooting British Major Pitcairn at Bunker Hill, June 7, 1775.

When Jones witnessed their loyalty, devotion, and courage, he declared, "I can no longer bring myself to a distinction based on color or misfortune." Jones freed all his slaves and stated, "They are prime seamen and behaved as well as white men."

In the Continental Navy, many men of African descent served on Revolutionary gunboats. One African American, Captain Mark Starlin of the Virginia Navy, was commander of the Patriot. Starlin was re-enslaved after the war, despite his heroic battle record. By the summer of 1778, hardly a ship sailed in the Continental Navy without an African American gunner, officer, helper, or seaman.

Custer, a black shipwright from Philadelphia, served in the Navy and participated in a raid on Tory pirates near Billingsport in 1778, where he cut off the head of one of the pirates. Custer brought this grisly trophy back to Philadelphia and proudly placed it on display in a Sansom Street tavern, where the head attracted much attention.

Pompey rendered invaluable service as a spy at Stony Point, New York, on July 16, 1779. Pompey also contributed to the victory of forces under General "Mad Anthony" Wayne, for whom Wayne, Delaware County, Pennsylvania is named. Agrippa Hull, said to be an African Prince, served Polish patriot General Thaddeus Kosciusko through the Revolution. After the war, when General Lafayette returned to America, he visited Hull at his Stockbridge farm in Massachusetts.

African American women in Philadelphia and elsewhere contributed to the cause of independence. The Philadelphia newspaper *The Packet* carried this story in 1778 about an unknown African American woman who visited American prisoners of war in the Walnut Street prison.

> A free Negro woman (who in the service of a gentleman of the City of Philadelphia, now…in the country) having received two hard dollars for washing, and hearing of the distress of our prisoners in the jail, went to market and bought some neck-beef and two heads, with some greens, and made a pot of as good broth as she could. But having no more money to buy bread, she got credit of a baker for six loaves, all of which she carried to our unfortunate prisoners who were much in want of such a supply. She has since paid the baker and says she never laid out money with so much satisfaction.

Humanity is the same thing in rich or poor, white or black. Indeed, many known and unknown persons of African descent served in Washington's Army and did their duty like their white compatriots. The following is an account of Isaac Jones, who was born about the year 1754 in Africa and died December 27, 1847, at the age of 94 years. Isaac Jones saw service during the Revolutionary War against England in 1776, and served almost the duration of the war.

After some period of service in the Continental Army, he lived for 50 years in Bucks and Montgomery counties earning his livelihood by sharpening knives for cutting paper, also as a wood sawyer. After being mustered out of the Continental Army, he was entitled to receive a pension. Someone for years had been drawing this pension for him but did not apply it for his benefit, so he spent his last short time on earth with Michael and Peter Mayer, who gave him a home. Jones' obituary was published in the *Reading Adler*, January 4, 1848.

Washington crossing the Delaware River on Christmas Eve night in 1776. With him was Prince Whipple, Washington's bodyguard, who is depicted in the boat pulling a stroke oar along with other soldiers.

Another Pennsylvania African American solider, John Emery of Philadelphia, served as a private in the Fifth Pennsylvania Regiment.

Oliver Cromwell was one of the many African Americans famous for crossing the Delaware in the middle of the night on December 25, 1776. Washington thought so highly of his tall and well-built bodyguard that at the end of the war he wrote his discharge in his own hand. Oliver Cromwell died in 1853. The Burlington, New Jersey, *Gazette* wrote of him on his 100th birthday.

Prince Whipple also participated in the crossing of the Delaware River on that cold Christmas Eve night to attack the Hessian soldiers in Trenton, New Jersey. Whipple, who was also Washington's bodyguard, is shown in two famous paintings of the crossing, pulling a stroke oar with other soldiers.

There were several all-black regiments in Washington's Continental Army. The Bucks of America, a Massachusetts regiment, rendered such valuable service that John Hancock gave them a special flag. After the war, the unit was honored with a special ceremony in Boston.

How many American textbooks tell the story of the all-black regiment from St. Dominique who fought the bloody Battle of Savannah, Georgia. Among this unit was Henri Christophe, the 12-year-old future king of Haiti. These brave men fought for America's independence. More than 200 years later their descendants were Haitian refugees known as "Boat People" who were denied entrance into this country.

VALLEY FORGE

Positioned in Montgomery and Chester counties is Valley Forge National Park, the site of George Washington's winter encampment. Historians have recorded the bravery of many white

Revolutionary War heroes; however, until recently, the deeds of African Americans soldiers who endured the cold winter of 1777-1778 have been overlooked.

Phillip Field of the 2nd New York Regiment died in Valley Forge because of the severe cold weather. Mentioned elsewhere in this book, Cyrus Bustill brought bread to the starving army, and Richard Allen brought salt and supplies from Rehoboth, Delaware, to Valley Forge. The 1st Black regiment came from Rhode Island. On January 2, 1778, General James Mitchell Varnum wrote General Washington, "It is imagined that a battalion of Negroes can easily be raised in Rhode Island." Washington

The First Rhode Island Regiment of African descent participated in several important battles of the war. While the Continental forces were encamped at Valley Forge, General George Washington sent General James Varum to Rhode Island to recruit African American soldiers. Later the regiment from Rhode Island were encamped at Valley Forge.

gave his endorsement and immediately dispatched Colonel Christopher Greene to attend to the matter.

African American volunteers were offered their freedom in exchange for service. By March 1778, a large unit of African American soldiers was encamped at Valley Forge. In June 1993, a stone monument standing 9'6" tall and 6' wide, entitled Patriots of African Descent, was erected at Valley Forge by the African American women of the Valley Forge chapter of Delta Sigma Theta sorority. The inscription on the monument reads: "Throughout these Historic and Hallowed Campsites were Courageous Black Patriots Who Participated in Our Nation's Bitter Fight for Independence." One of the most important African American soldiers at Valley Forge was Bristol Bud Samson of Susquehanna County. A memorial to him is being developed in Susquehanna County.

Many of the African American patriots who fought gallantly under fire could have joined British regiments, promised freedom if they fought against their masters. Many soldiers may have been enslaved by their American owners, but they chose to fight for their country. Many African Americans, both freed and enslaved, sided with the Loyalists and became Lord Dunmore's Ethiopian Regiment. They became political and military pawns of both armies including a number of African American women who, along with white women, took up with the British in Philadelphia as prostitutes.

The *Pennsylvania Evening Post* of December 14, 1775, reported one month after Dunmore's proclamation was issued that a "white gentlewoman walking near Christ Church was insulted by a black man. When she chastised him, he said defiantly, 'you d[amne]d white "B", till Lord Dunmore and his black regiment come, and then we will see who is to 'stay take the wall.'" The Dunmore proclamation forced the colonists to revoke an order prohibiting blacks from serving in the Continental Army.

British General Lord Dunmore mustered the first black regiment for Britain during the Revolutionary War. He is noted for his famous "Dunmore Proclamation." The Americans accused Dunmore of starting a race war. Southern whites, with their vast numbers of slaves, vigorously protested the loudest. General Washington wrote Colonel Henry Lee, December 20, 1775; "Success will depend on which side can arm the Negroes faster."

Alexander Hamilton and James Madison not only urged enlistment of slaves, but also argued in favor of their freedom in return for service under arms.

At the end of the Revolutionary War, when the Loyalists by the thousands left New York, New England, and other places along the eastern seacoast, hundreds of black loyalists took refuge in New Brunswick, England, and Canada. In London, July 1778, Ann Robinson offered a $20 reward for a servant Negro woman named Dinah.

> About 5'8" high, tawny complexion, about nineteen or twenty years old; had received a cut on the forehead from one of the soldiers shortly before she went away; was big with child and near the time of her lying in when she ran away with the last of the British troops from the city of Philadelphia.

Debra Newman Ham, an African American scholar, estimates that 27 African American woman from Pennsylvania left with the British and joined hundreds of others from other states. For instance, the National Archives and Record Service Papers of the Continental Congress provides the following examples:

> Flora Hill, ordinary wench, formerly property of James Yard, Philadelphia, left in 1778. Lucy Hart, 35, stout wench, formerly property of Sampson Levi of Philadelphia, who gave her her freedom and Sally Miles, 10, fine wench, formerly property of Philip Dickinson of Philadelphia, left six years ago.

Other women left with their husbands or other relatives. Many of these refugees were taken to Nova Scotia where they were given small land grants. Although a number of their descendants remain in Nova Scotia, many of their ancestors were shipped to Sierra Leone, in West Africa, because of Nova Scotia's harsh winters.

EDWARD (NED) HECTOR – BLACK SAMPSON OF BRANDYWINE

Paul Laurence Dunbar, an African American poet and one of America's most read poets during the beginning of the 20th century, immortalized Edward (Ned) Hector, a 33-year-old African American soldier from Conshohocken, Pennsylvania. Although George Washington's army was forced to retreat after the Battle of Brandywine, September 11, 1777, the defeat did not demoralize Hector. In his book *Myths and Legends of Our Land*, C.M. Skinner wrote," In the fight at Brandywine, Black Sampson, a giant Negro, armed with a scythe, sweeps his way through the red ranks."

Poet Dunbar captured the essence of the event by paying tribute to Edward Hector, whom many scholars believe was Black Sampson.

> Gray are the pages of record. Dim are the volumes of old; else had old Delaware told us more that her history held. Told us with pride in the story. Honest and noble are fine more of the tale of my hero, Black Sampson of Brandywine. Sing of your chiefs and your nobles, Saxon and Celt and Gaul, breath of mine ever shall join you. Highly I honor them all. Give to them all of their glory, But for this noble of mine, lend him a tithe of your tribute, Black Sampson of Brandywine. There in the heat of battle, there in the stir of the fight, Loomed he, an ebony giant. Black, as the pinions of night, swinging his scythe like a mower over a field of grains. Needless the care of the gleaners, where he had passed amain. Straight through the human harvest cutting a bloody swatch, woe to you soldiers of Briton! Death is abroad in his path. Flee while the moment is thine. None may with safety withstand him, Black Sampson of Brandywine. Was he a freeman or bondman? Was he a man or thing? What does it matter? His bravery, Render him royal, a king. If he was only a chattel, Honor the ransom may pay of the royal, the

loyal black giant, who fought for his
country that day. Noble and bright is
the story, worthy the touch of the lyre,
Sculptor or poet should find it full of
the stuff to inspire. Beat it in brass and
in copper, tell it in storied line, so that
the world may remember Black
Sampson of Brandywine.

Hector, a tall man with enormous strength, died at the age of
90 in 1834. Two Norristown, Pennsylvania, newspapers printed
his obituary. In a condensed form it reads:

Edward Hector, a colored man and vet-
eran of the Revolutionary War, exhibited an example of patriotism and bravery
which deserves to be recorded. At the
Battle of Brandywine, he had charge of
the ammunition wagon attached to Col.
Proctor's regiment and when the
American Army was obliged to retreat,
an order was given to abandon the
wagon to the enemy. The heroic reply of
the deceased was uttered in the spirit of
the Revolution: The enemy shall not
have my team. I will save the horses or
perish myself. He instantly started on
his way and proceeded. Amid the confusion of the surrounding scene, he calm-
ly gathered up arms which had been left
on the field by retreating soldiers and
safely returned with wagon and team all
in the face of the victorious foe.

One of Hector's contemporaries, John Francis, another
African American soldier from Pennsylvania, lost both of his legs

in the Battle of Brandywine. Hector's grave lies in Upper Merion Township near King of Prussia, Pennsylvania. A Pennsylvania State Historical Marker located at Hector and Fayette Streets in Conshohocken, Pennsylvania, honors his name.

DEBORAH SAMPSON GANNET—THE FIRST AFRICAN AMERICAN FEMALE SOLDIER

Many students of American history know the story of Molly Pitcher, a white woman who was a heroine of the Battle of Monmouth, New Jersey, June 28, 1778, in the Revolutionary War. Her real name was Mary Ludwig. John Casper Hays, her husband, enlisted as a gunner in the First Pennsylvania Artillery in 1775. He spent the winter of 1777 and 1778 at Valley Forge.

Like many soldiers' wives, and prostitutes, Molly was among the women who joined her husband in camp and made herself useful by cooking, washing, and doing other work around the camp. The Battle of Monmouth was one of the hottest days of a hot summer. Molly had followed the Continental Army to the battle and busied herself carrying water from a nearby spring in a pitcher to thirsty soldiers. From this episode, she got her nickname, Molly Pitcher. Her husband was wounded while firing his gun. Molly promptly took his place and fought the rest of the battle.

Another courageous heroine of the Revolution whose name is often omitted from history books was Deborah Sampson Gannet, an African American woman who enlisted under the name of Robert Shurtleff in the 4th Massachusetts Regiment in 1782 and served to the end of the war. Massachusetts gave Gannet as a reward 34 pounds sterling, praised her ability as a soldiers and for "at the same time preserving her virtue and chastity of her sex unsuspected and unblemished." It is said that Deborah Sampson Gannet exhibited an extraordinary instance of female heroism and her heroic deeds are recorded by African American historian William C. Nell's *Colored Patriots in the American Revolution*, published in 1855. Deborah donned her uniform for the Independence Day parade until her death in 1827.

One of the most spectacular women of enormous proportions from Georgia named Mammy Kate rescued Governor Stephen Heard from a British prison by carrying him out on her head in a huge basket covered with clothes. This incident is recorded in M.P. Andrews' *Women of the South in War Times*.

Thomas Fuller, born in Africa and held as a slave in Alexandria, Virginia, was known as "The African Calculator." He had an uncanny genius for mathematics. Fuller could neither read nor write; however he could calculate numbers involving millions in his head better then most men of his day with a pencil. Fuller could give rapidly the diameter of the Earth's orbit in inches. He could give the number of seconds in seventy years, odd months and days in ninety seconds including the leap year. Fuller died December 29, 1790, at age 80.

Another African-American woman, Hannah Till of Philadelphia, served as personal cook to George Washington and General Lafayette at Washington's headquarters in Valley Forge. She is remembered as being one of the few women connected to the historic encampment. When Lafayette returned to Philadelphia in 1824, he visited Hannah Till who was over 100 years old.

SIX

PHILADELPHIA'S AFRICAN AMERICAN LEADERS—ABSALOM JONES, JAMES FORTEN AND CYRUS BUSTILL

The Rev. Absalom Jones, born a slave in Sussex County, Delaware. Helped to organize the Free African Society in 1787. Founded St. Thomas African Episcopal Church in Philadelphia, Pennsylvania. Respected leader in Philadelphia's black and white communities.

Reverend Absalom Jones – A Man of Dignity and Commitment

*A*bsalom Jones' contemporaries describe him as quiet man, rather introspective, and as a mediator type. He was born a slave near Seaford, Sussex County, Delaware, on November 6, 1746.

Jones had been separated from his mother, four brothers, and a sister while still a young boy. In 1762, at the age of 16, he was taken to Philadelphia by his owner and employed as a stock clerk and handyman. Like several other enslaved Africans living in Philadelphia, he was allowed to work for himself.

Jones was ambitious and taught himself to read from a spelling book he bought with a few pennies and from the New Testament. Later his owner permitted him to attend night school. Jones worked overtime, saved his money, and married a slave woman whose freedom was purchased with the help of her father and a Quaker.

He later purchased several parcels of property in his wife's name and continued to save money to purchase his own freedom in 1784, and bought his own home and built two rented houses on the same property, which provided Jones extra income.

In the process of time, Jones became a friend of Richard Allen and together they founded the Free African Society in 1787, which served as a protective society and social organization for free African Americans. Disputes arose concerning leadership of the religious rites for the society, and Jones was awarded the post.

Jones and Allen, both inclined to preach, were part of St. George's Methodist Church. Harassed by the white Methodists, Jones and Allen made a decision to organize freed African Americans outside of the church and so the Free African Society was established. Jones and Richard Allen and other African Americans shared a humiliating experience at St. George's Church when Jones was literally dragged from his knees while worshipping.

Toward the end of 1790, Jones and Allen were encouraged by Benjamin Rush to inaugurate a separate black church. Jones believed that an African American church should be more than a place for religious worship. He stated that the church must promote education, mutual aid, and protest. In 1793, Jones began to build a church on Fifth Street below Walnut Street. It was opened on July 17, 1794. The name St. Thomas was used in the act of incorporation approved a month later after the dedication of the building.

Jones became its first rector, getting the approval of the diocese of Pennsylvania to conduct his ministry. The small, brick, church wall contained the following inscription, "The African Church MDCCXCIII. The people that walk in darkness have seen a great light."

Jones continued to work with other prominent leaders in Philadelphia's African American community such as Richard Allen, Cyrus Bustill, William Gray, and James Forten, who was a member of the St. Thomas vestry.

In 1798, the African Masonic Lodge was founded in Philadelphia and Jones was elected Most Worshipful Master and Richard Allen became the treasurer. In 1799, when George Washington died, Absalom Jones preached a commemorative service for the nation's first President. During the same year, Jones and 75 other African Americans sent a petition through a representative in Congress, Robert Wain, of Pennsylvania, who petitioned the United States Congress against the slave trade.

In 1808, Jones published *A Thanksgiving Sermon to Celebrate the Abolition of the Slave Trade* on the day the ban took effect, January 1, 1808. In 1814, when the British were threatening Philadelphia, Jones and Allen were called upon to recruit African American fighters. Some 2,500 men marched to Gray's Ferry and manned the defenses. When his friend Richard Allen was consecrated as the first bishop of the African Methodist Episcopal

Church on April 11, 1816, Jones participated in the ceremony. The Reverend Absalom Jones died in 1818.

The *Poulson's American Daily Advertiser*, an early Philadelphia newspaper, published the following advertisement Monday morning January 18, 1808:

African Episcopal Church Lottery

At a meeting of the Commissioners of the African Episcopal Church of St. Thomas Lottery, held Nov. 12, 1807, the following resolution was unanimously adopted: -

"Resolved, that the Commissioners will POSITIVELY Commence Drawing, On Tuesday the 24th inst. in the Statehouse; where the High Prizes will be put in the wheel, in the presence of several respectable citizens, who will be invited on the occasion."

Those persons, who are disposed to purchase Tickets, will please make early application to the commissioners or brokers, as the price will shortly be raised.

The Commissioners are determined to proceed with all possible dispatch to hold the drawing; and they flatter themselves from the number of Tickets already sold, that it will be concluded at an early period.

Samuel Wheeler, No., 99 Vine Street
Thomas Cumpston, 301 Market st.
Wm. Murdoch, 71 north Water st.
Joseph Bennet Eves, 103 Market st.
Peter Browne, 141 north Front st.

Ephraim Clark, 1 south Front st.
Daniel Smith, 181 south Third st.
Matthew Mc Connell
Wm. Blackburn
George Taylor
Michael Doran
James O'Ellers
Michael Fortune
W.M. Biddle & Co.

Nov. 16 {Volume XXXVII.} number 9.1

JAMES FORTEN—PATRIOT, ABOLITIONIST, HUMANITARIAN

During his lifetime, James Forten was one of Philadelphia's most influential citizens. He was born in 1766 into a free African American family. Forten once declared, "My great-grandfather was brought to his country a slave from Africa. My grandfather obtained his own freedom. My father never wore the yoke...."

During the American Revolution, at age 14, he joined Captain Stephen Decatur's crew on a vessel, the *Royal Louis*, serving as a powder boy. On his second voyage at sea, his vessel was captured. Forten and members of his crew were held captive on a British prison ship anchored off New York City. When an opportunity to go to England was offered by the friendly British captain who had captured the *Royal Louis*, Forten refused stating, "I have been taken for the liberties of my country, and never will prove a traitor to her interest."

He rendered valuable service to his country and emerged from the war a hero in Philadelphia and was employed as an apprentice to Robert Bridges, a sail maker in 1786. He became foreman of the sail loft and at the retirement of Bridges in 1798, Forten became owner of the company, located at 95 Wharf Street. By 1810, he was the leading sail maker in Philadelphia. He became known as an innovative craftsman.

Forten employed both black and white workers. One of Forten's contemporaries described him as " a Negro gentleman in possession of a fortune made by his own industry." It is estimated that his wealth exceeded $100,000, an enormous sum of money for any person at that time. He emerged as a leader in the African American community. Forten included among his friends Richard Allen, Absalom Jones, and Cyrus Bustill. He was active in a wide range of reform activities. He frequently spoke from the pulpit of Mother Bethel A.M.E. Church, and was one of the major movers who set up the First Colored Convention in Philadelphia in 1830.

Forten was especially prominent in the national and international anti-slavery movement, and led the protest against the American Colonization Society, which attempted to send free African Americans back to Africa. The Colonization Society was organized in 1816 in Washington D.C. as an alliance of missionaries and southern slaveholders. Its purpose was to find a satisfactory solution for the black problem by enforced emigration to Africa. Among its white supporters were Henry Clay, Andrew

James Forten, born of free parents in 1766. He served as a powder boy under Stephen Decatur during the Revolutionary War. Forten later became a wealthy sail maker and abolitionist as well as one of the most respected African Americans of his time.

Jackson, and Francis Scott Key, the author of the *Star Spangled Banner* and considered a friend of African Americans. When Jesse Torrey, Jr., a Philadelphia physician, attempted to aid a group of free blacks who had been kidnapped and placed in slavery, Key volunteered his legal services without charge.

Forten and his friend Richard Allen and other prominent leaders of the African Methodist Episcopal Church played an important role in a plan to send immigrants to Santo Domingo. According to the New York *Daily Advertiser* on September 24, 1824, the first group of 200 immigrants had left from Philadelphia and were the first to arrive in Samana. Early in December, the vessel Unity disembarked 100 immigrants and on the 22nd, Dr. Belfast Burton arrived with another group of immigrants from Philadelphia.

Forten was opposed to the Colonization Society's scheme, as were most African Americans, and called the scheme an attempt to get rid of free African Americans, making the institution of slavery more secure. Some African Americans such as New England ship owner Paul Cuffee, Forten's friend, believed that people of African descent could escape racism by establishing a government of their own in West Africa.

Cuffee, from New Bedford, Massachusetts, took 38 African Americans to Sierra Leone, West Africa, in 1812, paying all their expense so that they would have a better life.

Forten served as vice-president of the American Anti-Slavery Society. He became close friends with William Lloyd Garrison and loaned money to Garrison to start the *Liberator*, Garrison's famous anti-slavery newspaper. Forten's family and his son-in-law, Robert Purvis, were all active abolitionists. Poet John Greenleaf Whittier was a frequent visitor to Forten's large Lombard Street home.

Forten's sixth generation granddaughter, Charlotte, published a famous journal and after the Civil War taught former slaves in South Carolina's Sea Islands. During his life, Forten received a certificate of appreciation from the Humane Society for his rescue of four persons from drowning in the Delaware River on four different occasions. Among African Americans, Forten was one of the first to be noted as a major philanthropist. He died in 1842; 5,000 mourners, both black and white, attended Forten's funeral.

THE HOUSE OF CYRUS BUSTILL

An outstanding contemporary of early African American patriots along with James Forten, Richard Allen, and Absalom Jones, was Cyrus Bustill. His descendants are still living in the Philadelphia area. The Bustill family ancestry goes back more than

Robert Purvis, born free in Charleston, South Carolina. Purvis' father was a wealthy English merchant and his mother was a woman of African and Jewish heritage. Purvis was sent at an early age to Philadelphia, where he was to champion the cause of freedom. While attending Amherst College in New England, he met William Lloyd Garrison, whose writing influenced Purvis to devote his life to the liberation of African Americans. He married James Forten's daughter and published his famous "Appeal of Forty Thousand Citizens Threatened with Disenfranchisement of the People of Pennsylvania" in 1838. He was also president of the Philadelphia Underground Railroad.

116

John Greenleaf Whittier was a Quaker poet of bucolic verse who gave powerful voice to the spread of slavery. Whittier came from Massachusetts to Philadelphia to edit The Pennsylvania Freeman, *an anti-slavery newspaper. He included James Forten and his family among his African Americans friends.*

250 years in American history. The Bustills, who founded Burlington, New Jersey, in 1677 are a mixture of English Quakers, African, and Native American.

Cyrus Bustill, the most prominent of this family, was born a slave in Burlington, February 2, 1732. He learned the art of making bread from a well-known Quaker baker named Thomas Prior. Bustill bought his freedom. He always championed the cause of freedom and gave of his means to promote it.

He married Elizabeth Morey, daughter of Satterthwart, a Native American woman of the Delaware people. Bustill and his wife had a family of eight children: Rachel, Mary, Ruth, Leah, Grace, Charles, Cyrus, and David.

During the Revolutionary War, he baked bread for George Washington's army at Valley Forge. This was a patriotic contribution to the struggle of Washington's continental forces. According to family tradition, Bustill received a silver coin as a souvenir from General George Washington. Later he moved to Philadelphia and established a business at 56 Arch Street. His daughter Grace lived next door and operated a millinery store with the help of her mother, Elizabeth.

Bustill, Richard Allen, Absalom Jones, and James Forten were founders of the Free African Society in 1787. Although he was a Quaker, Bustill contributed funds for construction of St. Thomas African Episcopal Church. His children became Presbyterian when they refused to sit on segregated black benches while attending Quaker meetings.

One of Bustill's daughters, Grace, later helped to organize the Female Anti-Slavery Society in Philadelphia and became a distinguished teacher and lecturer. According to an account of Gertrude Bustill Mossell, a journalist and descendant of Grace Bustill: "Cyrus was driving his wagon along the high road at a time when it was the rule that if there were two wagons or carriages on the road going in the same direction, the vehicle driven by the

Black person would drop to the rear and let the other driver pull ahead. The dust from the road would blow back into the face of the person who was following. But Cyrus Bustill moved his wagon aside for no man. When a local Pooh-Bah on the road tried to force him to do so, Bustill did not yield his position, and as a follow-up measure, he refused to sell the man or anyone in his family the bread and cake they usually bought. Cyrus Bustill ate no man's dust. Equal rights was his credo."

When Bustill retired from baking, he opened a school for African American children in his home at Third and Green Streets. A number of his children and grandchildren were agents and conductors on the Underground Railroad, while others became teachers and artists. Among Bustill's descendants are artists Robert Douglass and David Bustill Bowser, educators Jacob C. White, Sarah Douglass and Paul Robeson, who from the 1920s through the 1940s was hailed as one of the world's great actors. Additionally, critics said Robeson had one of the greatest singing voices of the 20th century. He was also a brilliant scholar, champion athlete, and activist for human rights. Robeson's mother was Maria Louisa Bustill, Cyrus Bustill's great-granddaughter.

Cyrus Bustill is buried in a family plot on the site that once was his former Edge Hill Farm in Bustleton. The Bustill family genealogy is a monument to African American family stability.

SEVEN

THE FREE AFRICAN AMERICAN COMMUNITY: THE NATION'S CULTURAL CAPITAL

Olaudah Equiano captured as a young boy from Nigeria, West Africa. Equiano was owned by several masters who took him to various countries. In Philadelphia, a Quaker named Robert King owned him. His narrative won acclaim in America and in England, and helped the British government to abolish slavery.

hiladelphia's freed African American community, the largest and most vibrant African American community in the nation, brought about the creation of separate lifestyles. Despite the odds, this community mastered white values and added new twists of its own. Of all the people who inhabited the 13 rebellious American colonies during the era of the Revolution, people of African descent were viewed as the least likely to accomplish a lasting cultural and educational contribution to the nation. Yet, even then with all the odds against them, a group of highly talented individuals came upon the scene.

For instance, as early as January 1789, the Philadelphia newspaper The *American Museum* stated, "There is now in this city a black man of the name of James Derham, a practitioner of physics, belonging to the Spanish settlement of New Orleans, on the Mississippi. This man was born in a family in Philadelphia, in which he was taught to read and write and instructed in the principles of Christianity. When a boy, he was transferred by his master to the late John Kearsly Jr., of this city, who employed him occasionally to compound medicines, and to perform some of the more humble acts of attention to his patients.

"At the time of the Revolutionary War, Dr. Kearsly enlisted on the side of the British Army and 'donated' the services of his slave, Derham, to the medical unit of the 16th British Regiment." In 1781, James Derham was sold again to Dr. Robert Dove of New Orleans. Derham's medical experience continued to grow until 1783 when Dr. Dove, impressed by James' medical skills, gave him the title "doctor" and his freedom. With knowledge of French and Spanish, Dr. Derham was able to develop a large and successful practice and a specialty in tropical diseases that at the time were very prevalent in New Orleans. Derham lived until 1820.

Meanwhile, Olaudah Equiano, or Gustavus Vassa, as he was called, became one of the most eloquent voices of his time. Equiano was captured as a slave from his Igbo village in Nigeria as a young boy and served under several masters in the Caribbean and America. He was owned in Philadelphia by a wealthy Quaker merchant named Robert King. One of his masters named him Gustavus Vassa after the title of a popular Swedish play. In his classic book entitled *The Interesting Narrative of the Life of Qlaudah Equiano or Gustavus Vassa,* of 1789, he wrote, "One day when all our people were gone out to their works as usual, and only I and my dear sister were left to mind the house, two men and a woman sat over the walls, and in a moment seized us both and without giving us time to cry out or make resistance they stopped our mouths and ran off with us into the nearest woods." He was later sold into slavery and brought to the New World. Because of Equiano's intelligence, his Quaker owner, Robert King, trained him to be a clerk.

As he toiled to enrich his master in Philadelphia, he observed the misery of slavery in the city. After gaining his freedom, he settled in London and wrote his book. In his narrative, Equiano wrote that he had few illusions about the good life for a black freeman in America. His autobiography helped the British government abolish slavery in Great Britain and in other countries in Europe.

Prince Saunders became one of the most renowned educators, lecturers, and politicians of his day. Born in Vermont, he taught school in Haiti and in Philadelphia. Saunders won great respect in England with the aristocracy because of his eloquent learning and polished manners. He was a personal friend of King George IV.

Prince Saunders, a free African American who was born in Vermont, became a prized possession among the upper class in the Philadelphia African American community. Saunders came to Philadelphia in 1818 and became affiliated with St. Thomas African Episcopal Church. Previously, Saunders had continued his education in London where he became acquainted with two prominent British abolitionists, Thomas Clarkson and William Wilberforce, who were advocates of black freedom.

Saunders later emigrated to Haiti and became a confidant of the eminent black King Henri Christophe (who as a boy 12 years old fought in the Battle of Savannah, Georgia, for American Independence from England). Saunders vaccinated and taught the king's children. Christophe was so impressed with Saunders that he appointed him as his Minister of Education. In 1816, Saunders returned to London. During the same year, he edited and published the Haitian Papers. After publication of the 220-page volume, Saunders returned to Haiti. He was dismissed as minister by the furious king for

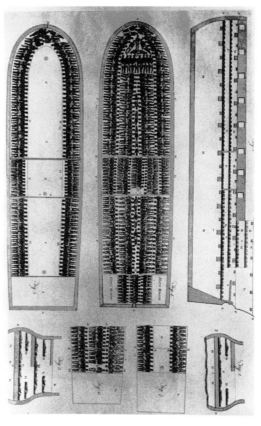

The interior of a slave ship published in English Abolitionist Thomas Clarkson's History of the Slave Trade *in 1808.*

having published the papers without permission. In Philadelphia, the ubiquitous Saunders wrote his first publication, an address delivered at Bethel Augustine Society for the Education of People of Colour, which was delivered on September 3, 1818. The members of the newly-organized society were so impressed by Saunders' eloquent address that they asked his permission to publish it.

Many white Philadelphians, however, were not impressed to generosity by these accomplishments and the accomplishments of other men and women of African descent. Instead the idea that African Americans were racially inferior to white people began to take hold with vicious force, and laws that governed the lives of free and enslaved Africans were made more repressive. Nonetheless, African Americans continued to organize cultural organizations such as debating societies and literacy societies. For example, William Whipper organized the Reading Room Society in 1828. Three years later, the Female Literacy Society was founded. Other intellectual and moral societies established in the city were the Minerva Literacy Association, 1834; The Library Company of Colored Persons, 1835; The Rush Library and Debating Society, 1836; the Edgeworth Society, 1836; The Demostheian Institute, 1837; and the Gilbert Lyceum, 1841.

Eleanor Harris is considered to be Philadelphia's first African American female teacher. Harris, a former slave who died in March 1797, was described as a "woman of character" and a well-qualified tutor of children.

Sarah Douglass is credited with being one of the first African American women to found her own school for black children. With a verbal license from Bishop Allen, Jarena Lee began to preach before integrated audiences along the eastern seacoast.

There is a long tradition in Philadelphia of African American women owning and operating businesses. A census of Philadelphia taken in 1795 lists seven African American women operating businesses, including five boarding houses keepers. "There is a record of the fact that in 1771, Sarah Noblitt was refused a license to keep a boarding house," said Dr. Henry M. Minton, an African American pharmacist in a March 13, 1913, speech entitled "Early History of Negroes In Business in Philadelphia."

THE FINE AND PERFORMING ARTS

From the earliest days of colonial America to the present time, African Americans have made invaluable contributions to Philadelphia's cultural life and to life beyond its borders. African slaves brought to this country were mostly inhabitants of West Africa, where the arts had developed a high degree of sophistication. Some of the qualities that served to refine the arts survived the terrifying trip to the colonies and provided America with its unique folk music and dance. Through poetry, songs, spirituals, and secular music, enslaved Africans and free persons expressed subtly, and not so subtly, their sorrow and secrets.

It was not until the Revolutionary War that craftsmen began to make substantial inroads into the various branches of the fine arts and crafts—silhouette makers, portrait painters, carpenters, blacksmiths, silversmiths, and furniture craftsmen were among the colonial African Americans who were motivated by pride of good workmanship and necessity.

Prosperous African Americans in Philadelphia who rejected dancing and other frivolities in favor of more serious intellectual activities were seen as vain, rich, and in many cases seem to have been emulating the activities of the white community, while at the same time accentuating class divisions. The structure was not, however, so rigid as to stop a higher class of African Americans from attending the African Fancy Ball.

125

The *Philadelphia Monthly Magazine* of April 15, 1828, provided its readers with a description of the ball. The following is a condensed version of the article:

As might readily be imagined, Cedar and New Market Wards, Southwark, Moyamensing, and Passyunk, were in great commotion upon the occasion. Never did Little Pine Street take so deep an interest in any event. From morning till night nothing was to be seen but belles and beaux bearing bundles of "costumes," second hand clothes rose fifty per cent,

Shown here is a couple dressed to the nines in colorful clothing to dance at the February 1828 African Fancy Ball.

and the gentlemen of the Three Golden Balls, licensed and unlicensed, made most unlicensed profits. There was no danger that the needles of Messrs. Appo and Sammons would rust for want of employment; and what advances was made in the price of perfumery, Mr. Cassey can best tell.

The twenty-eighth of February at length arrived. Happy the footmen and chambermaids whose masters and mistresses could dispense with their services all the afternoon and evening! Thrice happy they whose leave of absence was accompanied by the present of a pair of old silk stockings, or the loan of a past breastpin! The bootblacks with one accord closed their cellars, and there was not a porter to be seen in all Market-street. Showers of hair-powder began to fall in the vicinity of Shippen and Sixth-streets, at four o'clock.

The company began to assemble at half past seven, a curiosity to see the result of the Managers' arrangements overcoming the fashionable fear of being too early. To judge from the encomiums bestowed upon the effects of gentlemen's taste, never were Managers so successful. Upon the floor was pictured in charcoal a Map of Africa, and opposite the orchestra, shone a large transparency, designed by Mr. Quaminy Brown, representing in one part the Abolition Society benevolently breaking the shackles of the Negroes. In the centre appeared the Alms-House, with a distant view of the New Penitentiary, and the House Refuge;

whilst the left of the picture displayed a vessel about to sail to Liberia with cargoes of African embarking for their fatherland.

After dancing cotillions until twelve o'clock, lemonade and other light refreshments were handed to the ladies, whilst brown paper and sugar were burnt preparatory to the commencement of the waltzes, which lasted until three in the morning, when supper was announced. And now a difficulty arose which called all the conciliating abilities of the Managers into play. The Mustee ladies insisted upon sitting above the Mulattoes, and these asserted their right to take place above the Blacks.

A compromise was made upon the suggestion of Mr. Quaminy Brown, that the changes should be rung upon Black, Mustee, and Mulattoe, an arrangement which gave general satisfaction, as the supper was getting cold during the progress of the argument.

The cravings of hunger being allayed, waltzing was resumed, and kept up until five o'clock, when the company began to retire, highly pleased upon the whole with the amusements of the evening, and proposing, should their masters and mistresses approve of it, to let no winter pass in future without an African Fancy Ball.

One of the dances, "Patting Juba," included the use of hands patting various parts of the body while keeping rhythm with the feet. Only free African Americans who could trace their arrival in America at least one generation were permitted to attend the African Ball. The first ball was held in February 1828.

THE THEATER

African American theater in Pennsylvania and elsewhere in the United States was late in finding a legitimate foothold. Active development began in 1769, when a black character named Mungo appeared in the comedy *The Padlock*.

Several years later in 1776, African Americans appeared in John Leadock's *The Fall of British Tyranny*. However, the earliest recorded appearance of an African American on stage in Pennsylvania occurred during the same year, 1776, when an unnamed black actor played a minor role in Murdock's *Triumph of Love* at the Chestnut Street Theater in Philadelphia. Murdock also introduced the character Sambo to the American stage.

Black and white actors who performed in blackface prevailed into the 19th century as forces to be reckoned with in American theater. New York City's Ira Aldridge was acclaimed across Europe for the sensitivity of his portrayals, especially of Othello. Aldridge began his acting career with the African Company of Negro Actors in 1821. James Hewett of New York City is considered the first celebrated African American actor in the United States.

Ira Aldridge was an internationally known African American actor, who was born of slave parents in 1807 in New York. When he was 20 years old, he played Othello at the Royal Theater in London. There is an Ira Aldridge memorial chair in the Shakespeare Memorial Theater at Stratford-on-Avon in England.

Harriet Tubman, originally named Araminta, born a slave on a plantation in Maryland about 1820. She escaped to freedom in Pennsylvania in 1849. A legend in her times, again and again she risked the wrath of slave hunters making at least 18 perilous excursions to bring others to freedom. Included among her passengers were her parents, whom she conducted all the way to Canada. She always carried a pistol to ward off pursuers and opium to quiet crying babies. "I never ran my train off the track and never lost a passenger," she explained. Rewards for Tubman's capture mounted to $40,000.

Edwin Forrest, a native of Philadelphia, was one of the greatest white actors of his day. His blackface performance in *The Tailor in Distress* was praised as "the realistic representation of the plantation Negro." However, finding no white actress willing to blacken her face to play opposite him, Forrest was forced to relinquish the opportunity to a black washerwoman.

When the Walnut Street Theater opened in 1808, Rachel Lloyd, an enterprising African American entrepreneur, started a restaurant in the theater and continued there until she retired in 1850. Theater about African Americans often was inaccurate; when Harriet Beecher Stowe's famous novel, *Uncle Tom's Cabin* appeared in Philadelphia, Harriet Tubman stated to a fellow servant that she did not want to see the play. Working as a cook in a Philadelphia hotel to earn money for her Underground Railroad activities, she declared: "I haven't got the heart to go and see the suffering of my people played on stage. I've heard Uncle Tom's Cabin read, and I tell you Mrs. Stowe's pen has not begun to paint the picture of what slavery is at the far South. I've seen the real thing and don't want to see it on any stage or theater."

Mary Esparatero Webb, the wife of Philadelphia author Frank Webb, is reported to have been the first African American actress to perform on the legitimate stage. She appeared in short sketches and read portions of *Uncle Tom's Cabin* before audiences in London. She performed during the decades of the 1850s and '60s both at home and abroad. She was a relative of Charlotte Forten, whom she wrote quite often during her travels in various countries in Europe. She was also a friend of Lady Byron. Her husband, Frank, published in 1857 *The Garies and Their Friends*, the second novel published by an African American. The scene of the novel took place in Philadelphia prior to the Civil War.

Mary E. Webb, wife of Philadelphia author Frank Webb, is reported to have been the first African American actress to perform on the legitimate stage. Here, Webb is reading portions of Uncles Tom's Cabin *before audiences in London. She was also a friend of Lady Byron.*

LADIES OF THE NIGHT

The ladies of the night have a long and interesting history. One writer recorded that, "Prostitution along the waterfront had been strongly entrenched since William Penn's time and flourished in face of intermittent raids and fines."

The "City of Brotherly Love" itself has always had a reputation as a rather quiet, non-sexual sort of place until recent years. However, as early as the mid-1700s, Moreau de St. Mery, a French refugee from St. Dominique, a scholar and publisher who lived in Philadelphia for a short period, noted in *American Journey 1793-1798*, "The daughters of Quakers are extremely imprudent, and frequently get into trouble."

Quaker youth were frequent visitors in the houses of ill fame, which multiplied in Philadelphia and were frequented at all hours. There were streetwalkers of every color. St Mery said, "Since 1806, there were street walkers of a new sort in

Philadelphia. These are very young and very pretty girls elegantly dressed who promenade two by two, arm in arm and walking very rapidly, at an hour that indicates that they aren't just out for a stroll. They are found most commonly on the south side of Market Street beginning at Fourth Street and coming up this street. They pretend to be small dressmakers. They fulfill every desire for two dollars, half of which is supposed to pay for the use of the room."

A few words might be said about another curiosity connected with the ladies of the night. *A Guide to the Stranger of Pocket Companion for the Fancy, A List of the Gay Houses and Ladies of Pleasure in the City of Brotherly Love and Sisterly Affection,* was issued in 1849. The addresses listed were located in the most respectable parts of the city, known today as Society Hill. It is amusing to read that a certain Mrs. Nelson at Sixth and Pine streets had "everything comfortable for accommodation of married ladies, sly misses and their lovers."

The most notorious house of ill fame, according to the author, was located on South Street above Eighth — "There is a brothel occupied by a swarm of yellow girls, who promenade up and down Chestnut street every evening, with their faces well powdered and strange to say they meet with more customers than their fairer skinned rivals in the trade of prostitution."

Over 200 years ago, Moreau de St. Mery wrote in his journal, "The color prejudice is more deeply rooted in Philadelphia and in Pennsylvania than in the other states of the Union." Such discrimination has been prevalent in African American life for a long time.

For better or worse, people of African descent in Philadelphia have survived a long journey, a journey that represents strength and stability, lest anyone forget people of African descent in Philadelphia and elsewhere have an American history that pre-dates the words written on the Liberty Bell, "Proclaim

Liberty throughout the Land unto all the Inhabitants thereof," and the Declaration of Independence.

Philadelphia's black community represents a vibrant and diverse group of people. The United States census for the year 2000 indicated that there were 635,824 people of African descent living in Philadelphia. From the decade of the 1980s into the 21st century, there was a constant stream of immigration into Philadelphia by people of African descent from the Caribbean Islands, primarily from Jamaica, Barbados, Trinidad-Tobago, Haiti, Puerto Ricans of African descent, and the Virgin Islands. The English-speaking Jamaican and Barbados accent is markedly distinct from French-speaking Haitians with its mixture of Creole.

There are also a number of French-speaking African people from Martinique and Guadeloupe. However, immigrants of African descent have also settled in Philadelphia from Brazil, Costa Rica, Colombia, Ecuador, Honduras, and other Central and South American countries. A significantly large immigration from the continent of Africa can be found in various locations throughout the city, consisting of Nigerians, Liberians, Ethiopians, and Ghanaians. South Africans represent the majority of these residents, but there were also immigrants from Mali, Ivory Coast, Somalia, Senegal, Zaire and Kenya.

EIGHT

MISCEGENATION: AMERICA'S SCAR OF SHAME

Merriam-Webster dispassionately
defines miscegenation as

*"a mixture of races; ESP: marriage or
cohabitation between a white person and a
member of another race."*

D erived from the Latin words *miscere* (to mix) and *genus* (race), the term was coined in 1864 by David G. Croly and George Wakeman in their pamphlet *Miscegenation: The Theory of the Blending of the Races Applied to the American White Man and Negro.* The publication caused quite a stir among abolitionists, southern planters, and politicians. Why such shocked reaction? Certainly not because such racial mixing was unheard of. It was actually as much a part of plantation life as slavery itself. People were simply loath to bring such dirty linen into the open.

It was a subject so fraught with explosive feelings, on both sides, that society tried to ignore what many members casually accepted in private. Such shame is not such an old-fashioned virtue, either; even today, miscegenation is an issue so sensitive that many blacks and whites refuse to discuss it. But away from the glare of publicity, knowledgeable people admitted that such mixing was simply another part of everyday life. Southern white women, in fact, provide some of the most poignant examples of its effect. Mary Boykin Chestnut, wife of a senator from South Carolina wrote in her book *A Diary From Dixie* (1905), "They (Negro women) are not picturesque only in fiction do they shine. Those beastly beauties are only animals."

President James Madison's sister, for instance, once remarked to the Reverend George Brown, a Presbyterian minister in Virginia, that, "We Southern ladies are complimented with names of wives, but we are only mistresses of seraglios."

Frances Kemble, the celebrated British actress and abolitionist, after she divorced her husband, Pierce Butler, a wealthy Philadelphian who owned a large plantation in Georgia, wrote in her book *Journal of Residence on a Georgian Plantation*, "Any lady is ready to tell you who is the father of all the mulatto children in everybody's household but her own. These she seems to think drop from the clouds."

Thomas Jefferson, third President of the United States and

the author of the Declaration of Independence, sired a number of mulatto children by his dead wife's half sister. Thomas Callender, once a friend of Jefferson and later his critic, wrote in the *Richmond Recorder* in 1802: "By this wench Sallie, our President has had several children. There is not an individual in the neighborhood of Charlottesville who does not believe the story, and not a few who know it. The African Violet is said to officiate as housekeeper at Monticello."

Sally Hemings has been described by people who knew her as an attractive woman with "creamy near white skin and her hair lustrous and dark." Two of Thomas Jefferson's children with Hemings were said to have found refuge in Philadelphia and Washington D.C., where with the transient population they took new identities and their mixed racial heritage became lost.

Several descendants of Thomas Jefferson and Sally Hemings reside in Philadelphia in the present day. Thomas Jefferson, "the definitive American," was a brilliant man who had acquired all of the trappings of aristocracy. However, he also was a man with unresolved contradictions. Jefferson wrote the most eloquent arguments on the behalf of the rights of man. But he did not free his slaves during his lifetime.

THE GREAT RANDOLPH SCANDAL OF POST-REVOLUTIONARY VIRGINIA

This scandal is centered on Anne Cary Randolph, also called "Nancy," and her famous cousin, John Randolph of Roanoke, Virginia, who were lovers. This intriguing story involving honor, hate, sex, and murder was exposed by a house slave named "Old Esau," who told his master about the incredible melodrama that took place at the plantation mansion house called "Bizarre."

The Randolphs were one of the First Families of Virginia, a

genteel clan that owned sprawling estates and hundreds of slaves and took an active part in colonial politics. Thomas Jefferson and John Marshall were just two of their famous cousins. But the Randolphs acquired a less savory reputation. In 1792, a scandal tainted their name for good. On October 1 of that year, Richard Randolph's sister-in-law Anne Cary Randolph allegedly gave birth to a child. Slaves present at the birth claimed that Richard killed the child, depositing it on some old shingles, probably because, many of them assumed, he had also fathered it.

Richard demanded a trial to clear his name, hired John Marshall and Patrick Henry to defend him, and won the case. As rumors spread from plantation to plantation, one of the stories that began to gain more frequency was that the child was really killed because its father was black. From this incident emerged the term, "nigger in the woodpile." The term also referred to the slaves' gleeful interest in such gossip and indicated that they couldn't keep a secret.

In 1809, Anne Cary Randolph married Governeur Morris of New York, who was United States minister to France (1792-1794).

History certainly doesn't lack for other famous examples of such affairs. In recent years it has been recorded that Aaron Burr, a Revolutionary War hero who served as Vice President of the United States under Thomas Jefferson, sired two illegitimate children by a woman of African descent from Haiti, a daughter named Mary and a son, Jean-Pierre Burr. The son changed his first name to John. He was a talented artist, barber, and conductor of the Philadelphia Underground Railroad. Burr, who sometimes passed as a white man, rendered valuable service to the city's freedom network by assisting numerous runaways.

Aaron Burr was known to have had an eye for attractive women regardless of race or color. One of his mistresses, before she married, was the daughter of a Philadelphia innkeeper named Leonora Sansay —nee Hassall, also known as Eleanora, Mary,

Clara, Nora, and Madame D'Auvergne. She was known by many names and described as both brainy and vivacious.

After she married a French merchant in Philadelphia named Louis Sansay and accompanied her husband to St. Dominique (Haiti), she wrote a book entitled *Secret History: Or the Horror of St. Domingo, In a Series of Letters, Written by a Lady at Cape Francois to Colonel Burr* (1808). Her second book was *Zelica, the Creole* (1820), whose author was identified only as "American." Both books were based on Sansay's life; indeed, the character Clara, as she wrote to Aaron Burr, is herself, "that Clara you once loved."

Burr also was accused of having made romantic advances to Peggy Shippen Arnold, the attractive wife of traitor Benedict Arnold. She refused his advances.

Other famous men during Aaron Burr's time were themselves products of such dalliances or of mixed marriages of French and Creole. For example, mystery still shrouds the births of Alexander Hamilton, first Secretary of the Treasury, and John James Audubon, who became famous for his bird studies.

As early as the days of William Penn there were inter-racial relations. A white servant was indicted for this offense in 1677, and a tract of land bore the name "Mulatto Hill." In 1698, the Chester County Court of Pennsylvania laid down the principle that mingling of the races was not to be allowed. The matter went beyond this, for in 1722 a Pennsylvania woman was punished for abetting a clandestine marriage between a white woman and a Negro.

A few months thereafter, the Assembly received a petition from the inhabitants inveighing against the wicked and scandalous practice of Negroes cohabiting with white people. It appeared to the Assembly that a law was needed and they set about framing one. According to the law of 1725-26, they provided stringent penalties: "No Negro was to be joined in marriage with any white person whatever...."

The law was severe. Upon offending white people it imposed stringent penalties; but upon the free Negroes it bore much more heavily. Thus, if a free Negro man or woman married a white person, that Negro was to be sold by the justices of the Quarter Sessions as a slave for life. For a white person, the penalty was seven years servitude and a fine of thirty pounds sterling. If the offense was fornication or adultery, the free Negro was to be sold as a servant for seven years. The white person thus guilty was to be punished by whipping, imprisonment, or branding.

Thomas Branagan, writing about late 18th century Philadelphia in his book *Serious Remonstrances* (1805) said, "I visited different parts of Africa, South America, the chief of the West Indies Islands, and the Southern States; and I solemnly declare I have seen more white women married to and deluded through the arts of seduction by Negroes in one year in Philadelphia than for the eight years I was visiting the above place."

Dr. W.E.B. Dubois, an internationally known African American scholar who was of mixed racial heritage, mentioned in his classic book *The Philadelphia Negro* (1899), "Mulattos early appeared in the state, and especially in Philadelphia, some being from the South and some from up state. Sailors from this port in some cases brought back English, Scotch, and Irish wives and mixed families immigrated there at the time of the Haitian revolt."

Dubois was referring to one of the most interesting groups that evolved from such a mixed society, labeled the Cordon Bleu, a class of prosperous free persons of color who were products of French and African liaisons. Upon arriving in Philadelphia, many of these French-speaking families attended Old St. Joseph and St. Mary Catholic Churches, where separate masses were conducted for these free persons of color, known as *gens de couler.*

When Admiral Sir William Penn, father of William Penn, founder of the colony of Pennsylvania, captured Jamaica for the British in 1655, Oliver Cromwell, then Lord Protector of

England, saw the possibility of supplying white people for the settlement of Jamaica while ridding England of some of its "undesirable" population at the same time.

Irish vagabonds, condemned persons, and poor prisoners were shipped to Jamaica during the following years. While the Irish were not the only Europeans to occupy Jamaica, records of the period indicate that they became a majority.

The ensuring years brought a good deal of intermarrying resulting in a large population of Jamaicans with Irish names. Some of these black Irish, as they were called, migrated to the United States. The Latin Maurus, a poetic term for someone from North Africa, occurs in European language as Moor, More, Morien and many other forms. In addition, the term "blackamoor" was long used to mean Negro. In any case, the Moors of Europe have influenced all the great historical cultures, even France, Spain, and Italy, where some dark-skinned Italians in southern Italy for many years were called Guineas because of their dark complexion.

Yarrow Mamout, served as a spy for General Washington during the Revolutionary War. He refused to use his slave name and identified himself with his African ancestry. Because of his fame as a spy, artist Charles Willson Peale painted his portrait.

Many early, enslaved Africans kept their Moorish names while living in America, such as Job of Boonda, Africa. A narrative of his life was published in 1734. Job was held in bondage in Maryland until he obtained his freedom. Another Maryland enslaved African, Yarrow Mamout, a spy for the Continental Army, kept his Moorish name. Philadelphia artist Charles Wilson Peale painted Mamout's portrait. In fact, many American whites and blacks whose name is in the Moor family — such as Murray, Morris, Morel, Morelli, Morrison, Moreau, etc. — can assume there is Moorish blood connection somewhere in their ancestry.

Shortly before the ante-bellum period, some states created rigid class divisions between African people of mixed parentage strictly according to the make up of their parents. For example in 19th century New Orleans, the list goes from lowest class to highest as the amount of African blood declines proportionately from term to term.

Parents	Child
black and white	Mulatto
mulatto and white	Quadroon
quadroon and white	Octoroon
mulatto and mulatto	Cascos
mulatto and black	Sambo
sambo and black	Mango
octoroon and white	Mustifee
mustifee and white	Mustifino

In his book published in 1890, Calvin Fairbanks states that Patrick Henry, the Virginia statesmen and orator who delivered the famous "Give me liberty or give me death" speech had a black son named Melancthon.

Many years after Henry's death, miscegenation remained a subject that was heatedly debated among Americans. Even members of the South Carolina legislature were forced to recognize miscegenation as a fact of life. When they tried to raise the question by suggesting a Negro was any person with even a single drop of non-white blood, George Tillman objected, "Gentlemen, then we must acknowledge that there is not a full-blooded Caucasian on the floor of this convention."

THE BASTARDY CASE BOOK

Some records of early black and white admixture during slavery were kept in a document known as the *Bastardy Case Book*. These books were commonly used in Delaware and other states sometimes kept similar record copies, which are extant. The book records illegitimate children who are born of slave fathers and white mothers, white fathers and black mothers, and free African American fathers and white mothers.

Passing was another phenomenon of miscegenation. Many people of African descent, whose complexion was light enough to cross over into the white world, passed for various reasons, some out of shame and others for special advantages. Several of Thomas Jefferson and Sally Hemings' children entered the white world, as did several members of the well-known Philadelphia abolitionist Robert Purvis family of Charleston, South Carolina, Philadelphia, and New York.

EARLY NAMING PRACTICES OF ENSLAVED AFRICAN PEOPLE

Since the days of their captivity and subsequent arrival in the United States, enslaved Africans were aware of the importance of their names only as they were able to make a mark, perhaps an

"X." For many enslaved persons, the second immediate response to freedom was to change their names. Most wanted to shed their masters' surnames or to shed classic names like Caesar, Pompey, Cudjo, Minerva, or Venus. Other common names were Cuff, Mingo, Congo, Cato, Jupiter, Paris, Jude, Little Buck, and even Uncle Remus. When freed, many persons of African descent discarded their slave names and adopted the names of their choice.

Sometimes the offspring of mixed marriages achieved prominence in their community, such as Jeremiah Shadd. Through his trade as a butcher and by acquiring real estate, Shadd became one of the wealthier African Americans in Wilmington, Delaware. He was the son of a white man; his mother was Elizabeth, or "Black Betty," Jackson, the wife of Gabriel Jackson, the noted ship carpenter.

Jeremiah was light-skinned enough to pass for white; however, he maintained his African identity and married Amelia Siscoe, a woman of French and African descent from St. Dominique who had settled in Wilmington after fleeing the revolt on the island during the early 1770s.

Many other immigrants of African descent had arrived on French vessels in the Delaware River from Martinique, Guadeloupe, and other French West Indian islands. Abraham Shadd, a relative of Jeremiah, attended the first Colored Convention in 1830 at Mother Bethel Church in Philadelphia. He also became a noted abolitionist and Underground Railroad agent in Wilmington and later in Pennsylvania.

Another prominent member of the family was Sally Shadd, affectionately called "Aunt Sally," who some claim introduced ice cream to Delaware.

By 1830, members of the Shadd family left Wilmington to settle in West Chester, Pennsylvania. Abraham's daughter, Mary Ann Shadd, was perhaps the most illustrious member of the family, an orator, schoolteacher and abolitionist. She was a tall, attractive, intelligent, and outspoken woman who became the first African American woman in North America to establish and edit a weekly newspaper, *The Provincial Freedman*, in Windsor, Canada.

African American orator and historian William Wells Brown described Mary Ann Shadd this way: "She is tall and slim with a fine head, which she carries in a peculiar manner. She has good features, intellectual countenance, bright, sharp eyes, that look right through you. She holds a legitimate place with the strong-minded women of the country. She earlier took a lively interest in all measures tending to the elevation of her race and has at various times filled the honorable positions of school teacher, school superintendent, newspaper publisher and editor, lecturer, and traveling agent. As a speaker, she ranks deservedly high; as a debater she is quick to take advantage of the weak points of her opponent, forcible in her illustrations, biting in her sarcasm, and withering in her rebukes. Although she has mingled in the society of men, attended many conventions composed almost exclusively of males, and trodden paths where women usually shrink to go, no one ever hinted aught against her reputation, and she stands with a record without blot or blemish. Had she been a man, she would probably have been with John Brown at Harper's Ferry."

While living in Philadelphia, Mary Ann became the Rosa Parks of her day when she refused to give up her seat and leave the city's segregated trolley

William Wells Brown former slave, Underground Railroad agent, anti-slavery orator, writer, playwright, and historian.

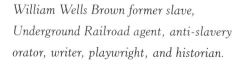

cars. Nothing was done to correct the situation until the Pennsylvania state legislature, not particularly sympathetic to African Americans, but less sympathetic to Philadelphia, passed a law ordering streetcar lines to permit the riding of African Americans.

Because of their anti-slavery and Underground Railroad activities, the entire Shadd family moved to Canada after the passage of the infamous Fugitive Slave Law of 1850. After the Civil War, Mary Ann Shadd-Cary (she married in Canada) returned to the United States, settled in Washington, D.C., and became one of the nation's first African American woman lawyers.

African American authors Gerri Majors and Doris Saunders stated in their book *Black Society*, published in 1976, "The Syphax family of Washington and Alexandria, Virginia, had its beginning in Alexandria on the Custis estate, when the grandson of Martha Custis Washington, George Parke Custis, fell in love with his grandmother's slave maid, Arianna, who was herself a product of miscegenation."

In 1857, the huge 1,100-acre Custis-Lee estate was deeded to one of Martha Custis Washington's descendents, William

Mary Ann Shadd-Cary, daughter of a prominent African American agent in the Wilmington, Delaware, Underground Railroad. The Quaker-educated teacher moved to Canada, assisted John Brown in mapping out plans for his raid on Harper's Ferry. She later edited The Provincial Freeman, *an anti-slavery newspaper, while still living in Canada. She preached permanent emigration from the United States.*

Henry Fitzhugh Lee, the second son of General Robert E. Lee. According to oral tradition, General Lee expressed fondness for an elderly African American woman, one of his former slaves, when he visited her in Chambersburg, Pennsylvania. During the time, he purchased his favorite horse, Traveler. A portion of Chambersburg was set fire by Lee's Confederate Army as his forces marched towards Gettysburg during the Civil War. There are many African American Lee families in Virginia, since so many former slaves took the surname after General Richard Henry Lee, the Revolutionary War hero and an ancestor of Robert E. Lee.

Frederick Law Olmsted, the designer of New York City's Central Park and an author, wrote in his book *A Journey in the Seaboard Slave States* (1856), "Jefferson Davis, President of the Confederacy, and every southern man in his memory runs back to the Negro woman who nursed him and as he grew to manhood the cordial welcome given him by his nurse, with tenderness scarcely inferior to his own mother." According to the report of Colonel Eaton, Superintendent of the Freemen Department of Tennessee and Arkansas for 1864, published in 1865, "Jefferson Davis had as his mistress, his mulatto niece, daughter of his own brother, Joe Davis."

William Wells Brown, another example of race mixing and a former slave, has the triple distinction of being the first African American novelist, dramatist, and author of a travel book. He earned the reputation of a historian, prominent anti-slavery orator, and agent on the Underground Railroad.

Brown, who could have passed for white, was born a slave in Kentucky in 1816. His childhood was spent on a plantation. After escaping from several slave owners, he eventually attained his freedom and educated himself by reading books and listening to abolitionist speakers. In 1844, Brown accepted a position as an agent for the Western New York Anti-Slavery Society. One year after

Harriet Beecher Stowe published her successful book *Uncle Tom's Cabin*, Brown published the first novel by an African American author in 1853, *Clotel* or *The President's Daughter*, which was based upon Thomas Jefferson's alleged slave daughter. The rumor of Jefferson's slave daughter had been circulated by abolitionist William Lloyd Garrison and published in his newspaper *The Liberator*, with a heading that read, "Jefferson's Daughter had Lately Been Sold for $1,000 on the New Orleans Market."

Brown's popular novel appeared in three editions. William Wells Brown states that his maternal grandmother was a descendent of Daniel Boone. When he visited Philadelphia in 1854, he said that Philadelphia's "colorphobia" was more rampant than that in pro-slavery New York City. Brown once stayed in the Pennsylvania home of abolitionists James and Lucretia Mott, and spoke before other friends at an Anti-Slavery Fair in West Chester, Pennsylvania.

William Lloyd Garrison, a native of Massachusetts, was one of the earliest and most vitriolic abolitionists. He devoted full time to the cause of speaking against slavery and the Constitution that permitted it. By 1841, he was calling for the North to secede from the Union. He founded and became editor of his famous anti-slavery newspaper, The Liberator.

Listed among Brown's other anti-slavery friends was Jane Grey Swisshelm, a renowned newspaper journalist for Horace Greeley's *Tribune*, an abolitionist and nurse during the Civil War. Swisshelm was noted for her sharp-witted writing style. While working in Washington, D.C., she was shocked at the miscegenation she saw everywhere, and especially in high places.

Swisshelm wrote in her book *Half Century* (1880), "While abolition was scoffed at by hypocritical priests of our most prominent statesmen in open concubinage with Negresses, adding to their income by the sale of their own children, one could neither go out nor stay indoors without meeting indisputable testimony of the truth of Thomas Jefferson's statement, 'the best blood of Virginia runs in the veins of her slaves,' but the case which interested me most was a family of eight mulattoes bearing the image and superscription of the great New England statesman, who paid the rent and grocery bills of their mothers as regularly as he did those of his wife."

Although inter-racial marriages and relations between white women and persons of African descent is quite prevalent today, in the early years of colonial America, it was forbidden as an act against social conventions.

Lucretia Coffin Mott, who was born on Nantucket Island in Massachusetts in 1793, and was a very educated Quaker wife and mother. Like her friend Harriet Tubman, she was a small woman who also was connected to the Underground Railroad with her husband James. She stood with William Lloyd Garrison for immediate emancipation for slaves. She was a friend of Frederick Douglass and a pioneer in the Women's Rights movement and also housed John Brown's wife while her husband's body was transported through Philadelphia.

Helen T. Catteral recorded in volume number 5 of her monumental works *Judicial Cases Concerning America and the Negro* (1929-1937), "In August 1692, in Maryland, a rich man's daughter was convicted of having too much commerce with a certain Negro and of having had a child by him. She was fined 6000 pounds of tobacco."

Sometimes the offspring of miscegenation founded entire communities, such as Gouldtown in New Jersey. Many of the people of Gouldtown are descendents of John Fenwick, Lord Proprietor of New Jersey. In the 1670s, one of the Fenwick heiresses, Elizabeth Adams, married a black servant. Her grandfather, John Fenwick, threatened to cut her off from the family wealth unless the Lord opened her eyes to see the abominable transgression against his name and her good father by giving her true repentance and forsaking that black which had been the ruin of her. There is no evidence that she ever repented. Many Gouldtowners have achieved prominence in African American society throughout the years and quietly melted into the white population.

John Chavis represents another remarkable example of achievement connected with New Jersey. He was born in 1763 in North Carolina, served in the Revolutionary War, and was educated privately at Princeton University in an experiment to see whether a full-blooded African American could absorb a college education. He succeeded and, after leaving Princeton, opened a private school for the sons and daughters of the wealthy in North Carolina and became a licensed Presbyterian minister. Princeton University did not permit African Americans to enroll at the university until nearly 150 years later.

When Woodrow Wilson was president of Princeton, he would not permit African Americans to attend the university, including scholar, singer, and actor Paul Robeson and his brilliant older brother, who lived a few short blocks from the university.

The Marquis (General Lafayette) made his triumphant

return to the United States in 1824 after 40 years. He was amazed to see how much lighter in complexion the African American population had become. Lafayette had always expressed liberal views toward people of African descent. On February 5, 1783, the Revolutionary War hero had written to George Washington asking him to set aside land for African Americans. In a letter to English abolitionist Thomas Clarkson, Lafayette declared, "I would never have drawn my sword in the cause of America if I could have conceived that thereby I was founding a land of slavery."

However, most scholars of American history fail to record a scandal that tainted his honorable name. In a letter sent to William C. Nell, a well known Boston African American abolitionist and author from Philadelphia dated February 22, 1848, he stated, "A circumstance that occurred about twenty-three years ago in the city of my birth and the birthplace of our fathers, I mean the Land of Chivalry, Charleston, South Carolina, may perhaps be interesting to your readers. Behold a natural son of General Lafayette, with a family of children, are slaves in our midst: the love of liberty from the father has descended to the son, he desires to be free and yet more, if possible, desires that his children, those little ones which God gave him, might be considered his own, he reflects, he determined if possible to obtain an interview with his father. The resemblance alone (although he had other evidence) is sufficient to establish the relationship. He is more like the General than his son, George Washington Lafayette. Never, indeed, were father and son alike. Not only did the father descend to an untimely grave, but his children the grand children of General Lafayette were held as slaves and as late as the year 1845 were subjected to the scourge and tyranny of a cruel master."

NINE

EARLY VENDERS, CATERERS AND RESTAURATEURS

The Pepper Pot Woman, among the most interesting street venders at Head House Square in Philadelphia. As they sold their soup, their cries could be heard above all other venders. "Pepper pot, all hot, all hot makee back strong, makee live long, come and buy my pepper pot."

$\mathcal{A}$lthough people of African Descent were active in many trades in early Philadelphia, one of the most long-standing was food vending. From the very beginning, enslaved and freed African Americans would tolerate no nonsense about food. A typical gathering place was the open market place of Head House Square. A recreation of that market area is located now at Second and Pine Streets.

Head House Square visitors and citizens of Philadelphia could hear melodious cries of food venders and those of other craftsmen calling out, "Hominy man, come out today, for to sell his hominy. Hominy man is on his way for to sell good hominy!" "Sea Bass! Fine Sea Bass!" "Hot Corn! Hot Corn!" "Watermelons, come and buy my ripe red watermelons!" and the White Wash could be heard calling out, "Yeres the White Whitey-Wash! Brown Whitey Wash! Yellow Whitey Wash! Green Whitey Wash! Wash! Wash, Wash! I'm about!"

The chimney sweeps had their own cries as they walked through the cobblestone square with long poles with a bundle of brushwood tied to the end of the cord. Among the most interesting street venders were the pepper pot women. These women of African descent often wore golden earrings and colorful kerchiefs upon their heads and a colorful wrap around their shoulders. On brisk autumn and winter days, their cries could be heard above all. "Pepper pot all hot! all hot!, makee back strong, makee live long. Come and buy my Pepper pot!" The recipe for Pepper Pot soup consisted of: 1 knuckle of veal or beef, 1 pound plain tripe, bunch of soup herbs, 1 large onion, 2 potatoes of good size, 1 bay leaf, 3 quarts of water, 1/2 pound suet for dumplings, 2 tablespoons butter, 2 tablespoons flour, salt and cayenne to taste --flour and seasonings for dumplings. Oystermen could also be seen offering their fare to hungry visitors.

On Sundays, African Americans of various social classes took advantage of the day set aside for worship and relaxation. On that day, they donned their finest clothes, women put on their brightest dresses and their prettiest shoes. Beautiful, exotic looking coffee and cream complected women of French, Spanish, and African descent, newly arrived from the Caribbean Islands, dressed richly in French and West Indian fashions with colorful turbans upon their heads, escorted by wealthy French gentleman, could be seen strolling through the open market square.

There was another popular market place located on Callowhill Street, between Front and Second Streets, made up of four buildings, running in the same direction as Head House Square. There were some restrictions, however, and generally, African Americans were not permitted to set up stalls or shops in

Colonial street vendors in Philadelphia

"Hominy man come out to-day
For to see his hominay
Hominay man is on his way,
for to sell his goog hominay"

"Sea Bass!
Fine Sea-Bass!"

"Pepper-pot!
All hot! all Hot!
Makee back strong
Makee live long!
Come buy my Pepp

major shopping or marketing areas that competed directly with white artisans or merchants.

Because ovens were rare in post-colonial Philadelphia homes of modest means, many African Americans established bakeries. George Brown in Parham Street; Randolph U. Campbell, Bedford below Twelfth; Daniel D. Fox, Passayunk Road below South; Risdon D. Hainesley, 7th below Shippen; Isaac Howy, Twelfth above Shippen; James Miller, 27 Prune Street; Alfred Rouker, Eagle Court; John Turner, Hog Alley; and James Wilson were all engaged in community baking. Their deliveries were made either by covered basket or small pushed handcarts.

"Split wood!
Split wood!"

"Hot Corn!
Hot Corn!"

"Y'ere's the White Whitey-Wash
Brown Whitey-Wash!
Yellow Whitey-Wash!
Green Whitey-Wash!
Wash, wash!
I'm about!"

THE CATERERS AND RESTAURATEURS.

Historically, it is important to set the record straight and emphasize the contribution of African American caterers and restaurateurs when they came on the culinary scene more than 200 ago. Many decades before Philadelphia's Old Original Bookbinder's and other modern five-star restaurants, the culinary profession in Philadelphia was dominated by a small group of African Americans caterers and restaurateurs who received international acclaim for their culinary expertise.

The best and most elegant service of food at balls, parties, and cotillions was provided by African Americans, and most of these establishments were located in Philadelphia's historic Society Hill.

Samuel Fraunces, or "Black Sam" as he was affectionately called, was Washington's personal cook in New York City. Fraunces owned a popular restaurant called Fraunces Tavern. After Washington's inauguration in New York as President of the United States, he appointed Fraunces as steward of the executive household, which transferred to Philadelphia. Fraunces was probably also present at the Germantown White House. When Fraunces operated his tavern in the Wall Street section of New York City, Washington and his officers used to dine there and discuss important revolutionary plans. After serving as President George Washington's personal steward of the executive home in Philadelphia, Fraunces opened another restaurant more elegant than his famous Fraunces Tavern in New York City.

Before Fraunces' first true restaurant—and the one he later established in Philadelphia—most places were private and restricted clubs for the rich and titled—except for some alcoholic drinking places and coffee houses mainly for men. The only other such prominent restaurant existing in the Western World opened in London in 1714. It was called Simpson's Fish Dinner House.

France opened the LeGrande Taverne de Londres in Paris in 1765. [This was before late-coming Maxims in Paris, the Waldorf in New York and Bookbinders in Philadelphia—places most culinary arts circles credit for true culinary arts beginnings and inventions.]

The pioneering culinary creations of President Washington's African American cooks and chefs are monumental. The demanding tastes of heads of state and visiting dignitaries in a changing environment where food products was the central theme insured that they were the first to serve or create many new dishes. They served the first ice cream at our nation's First House and formulated their own unique recipes of it. It was these African American cooks and chefs who popularized the creation of ice cream, and not Dolly Madison, whom some historians credit.

Fraunces was paid about $1,500 a year and all provisions and supplies for the Philadelphia White House. According to writings of that period, everybody liked "Black Sam." He was much darker than he appeared in portraits. On top of his gray, curly hair with a powdered wig, he wore a cocked hat when dressed for Sunday meetings, but in the marketplace he chose a round one.

Dapper and urbane, Fraunces had an aura of elegance about him. He could select from 21 ruffled shirts, 14 cravats to be fastened with a breast pin, and nine bright bandanna handkerchiefs, a waist coat from which dangled seals and fobs attached to his gold watch, a dark coat with gold buttons, and breeches fixed in place by silver buckles. On cold days, a flowing cape enveloped his figure.

After more than five years as steward of the executive mansion, Fraunces resigned and opened a restaurant referred to as "Tavern Keeper," located at 166 South Street, than moved the next year to South Water Street and named it "The Golden Tun Tavern." Since George Washington and other dignitaries dined at the tavern, it also drew foreign diplomats, merchants, and sea captains. A man of taste, fond of display and a connoisseur of wines, Fraunces catered to high society. Aristocrats dined there and large banquets were given. It might be of interest to note that the private dining room was well appointed, there was a large assembly room that could be rented for social functions, and the comfortable bedrooms were important parts of this hostelry. The furniture was extremely handsome and all of expensive, brightly rubbed mahogany, while sparkling chandeliers hung from the ceilings.

Fraunces died a few months after this establishment was opened in Philadelphia in 1795. He became a legend during his lifetime. A Pennsylvania State Historical Marker located at 310 South 2nd Street honors the former Fraunces Tavern. Heartbroken and forlorn, he left a will that stated that the federal government and several states owed him money for housing and feeding soldiers during the Revolutionary War.

St. John Appo established his firm at 6th and Spruce streets as early as 1804. His French Creole wife is alleged to have had an original recipe for ice cream that was the *specialite' de maison*. Their sons, William and Joseph Appo, played in Frank Johnson's band and orchestra at the Walnut Street Theater as early as 1824.

Frank Johnson of Philadelphia was the leading African American musician of his day. In England, Johnson's orchestra performed before Queen Victoria. He was a friend of General Lafayette.

Robert Bogle was the originator of the catering profession and the first African American to gain prominence in the field that was the first business in which Philadelphia's African Americans achieved affluence. Bogle's specialty was meat pies and soups. He also performed as master of ceremonies at weddings and funerals for his wealthy clientele. One of these clients, Nicholas Biddle, the prominent Philadelphia banker, wrote "An Ode to Bogle," a verse in Bogle's honor in 1829. As for Bogle, no party, ball, or large formal dinner was a social event unless under his direction. Bogle died in 1837, and is buried in Eden cemetery.

Peter Augustine, a French West Indian refugee of African descent from Haiti whose restaurant was located at 1105 Walnut Street, celebrated the reputation as the "Delmonico of Philadelphia." Augustine set a standard that was emulated by other caterers. The best families of the Philadelphia elite and the most distinguished foreign guests, including the Marquis de Lafayette, dined at the Augustine establishment.

Augustine purchased the former business of Robert Bogle and placed a plaque in front of his restaurant reading: *"Enter: Philadelphia French Haute Cuisine Gourmet Catering –1815-."*

Peter Albert Dutrieulle, another African American "Old Philadelphian," for years conducted a thriving business as a caterer and restaurant owner founded in 1875 and located in Center City. He operated his successful restaurant at 40

Robert Bogle of Philadelphia is linked intimately with the history of catering in America. He was the leading caterer of his day. Wealthy Philadelphian banker Nicholas Biddle wrote a verse in Bogle's honor, "An Ode to Bogle," in 1829.

South 15th Street. Before his death, he served as the president of the Philadelphia Caterers Association. After his death, his family members expanded the business with the Baptiste family, who were originally from the Caribbean Islands. Augustine Baptiste, another Haitian refugee, operated a refined establishment on South 15th Street.

James Prosser was another prominent early African American caterer and restaurateur who operated an oyster cellar that stood at 806 Market Street. However, the main labor of Prosser was cooking terrapin, a North American fresh water turtle, famous for its edible flesh.

Thomas Dorsey was a former Maryland slave who was aided by the city's Underground Railroad. He established himself as one

Specialties of African American venders and caterers were fresh clams and oysters. In the lithograph of the Oyster House by James Akin from the Philadelphia Taste Displayer or Bon Ton Below Stairs, *published 1825, white citizens enjoy samples of oysters as the proud African American chef looks on in delight.*

A Philadelphia Oyster Barrow, in front of the Chestnut Street Theatre from 1814 water color by Pavel Petrovich Svinin courtesy of the Roger Fund, Metropolitan Museum of Art, New York.

of Philadelphia's caterers with an establishment located at 1231 Locust Street. In 1875, a directory listed Dorsey as one of the wealthiest African Americans in Philadelphia. Dorsey assumed the role of leadership of the African American caterers and formed "The Guild of The Caterers."

Henry Jones and Henry Minton were also distinguished food merchants who operated an elegant dining room. Henry Minton was a master caterer preparing with perfection dishes of lobster salad, chicken croquettes, deviled crabs, and terrapin soup. All was considered the epitome of good eating during the era between 1845 and 1875.

Following Jones and Minton were John Holland, who operated a prosperous business in Center City. After his death, William Newman purchased the business. The former Holland/Newman business was acquired by John C. Trower and was located at 1526 Pine Street.

Augustus Jackson operated a successful confectionery business during the mid- 1800s selling ice cream. For years he enjoyed a monopoly on the sale of this tasty dessert. His establishment was located on Goodwater Street, now St. James, between Seventh and Eighth streets.

Many French-speaking families who arrived in America between 1793 and 1796 settled in cities such as New York, Philadelphia, Baltimore, Wilmington, Charleston, and New Orleans. Descendents continue to carry French surnames, such as these in Philadelphia: Alcindor, Abele, Appo, Cuyjet, Dutrieulle, Baptiste, Montier, Barthomew, Quad, Duterte, Le Count, and Roland.

The Roland family is related to Edward de Roland, a musician and composer who played in Frank Johnson's nationally known band and orchestra during the mid-1800s. These families later married into other prominent African American families who could trace their heritage in Philadelphia as early as the mid 1700s, calling themselves "Old Philadelphian."

In Wilmington, Delaware, John Garesche, a refugee, became a prosperous real estate owner. Another prominent family in Wilmington with a French connection was the George Fisher family, of Irish and African decent. Fisher married Pauline Conklin, who herself was a blood relative of Pauline Bonaparte, the wife of Napoleon. She was born in Martinique. George Fisher's son Orpheus married internationally-known concert singer Marion Anderson, "The Lady from Philadelphia."

In New York City, where a Caribbean colony had earlier gained a foothold with Samuel Fraunces' Tavern, Theodore Duplessis, another refugee, acquired wealth and became famous for his superlative ice cream.

African Americans owned and operated a number of other businesses in and around the Society Hill section of Philadelphia. Jane Brown, the daughter of Bishop Richard Allen, was refused a license in 1771 to keep a boarding house because of racism. Lucy

Johns was another early African American entrepreneur connected with Philadelphia. She had a millinery shop on Samson Street during the Revolution. Johns is known to have employed as many as 15 assistants when busy in preparing the frill and furbelow which was popular among women of that day.

Pierre Toussaint, another refugee from Saint Dominique, became one of the wealthiest and most prominent hairdressers in New York City. His Chapel Street location attracted visitors both domestic and foreign. Being a Catholic, Tousssaint in 1841 gave a large donation for the construction of St. Peter's Catholic Church, now St. Vincent de Paul. A number of African American hairdressers throughout the colonies adopted Toussaint's method and applied them to their clients.

Tailoring was another business that African Americans still own today. Cuff or Cophy Douglass, who married Phoebe Loom at Old Swede's Church in 1777 and lived until 1784, operated a successful tailoring business at 117 Elfreth's Alley, the oldest street in the nation, located off Second Street between Arch and Race Streets. Except for several members of prominent families, African American women worked outside of their homes as teachers, caterers, laundresses, scrubwomen, seamstresses, and lecturers. Hetty Reckless was connected with the Underground Railroad and worked with prostitutes as a moral reformer.

A number of African American women were well-known dressmakers during this period, beginning with Juliana Allmond; Elizabeth, Mary, and Sarah Venning; Mary Ann Gibbs; Delphane Alzier; Sarah Beulah; June Le Count; Harriet Nickens; Emeline Truitt; Mary Proctor; and Emeline Cornish. The name of Mary Burr should also be included. She was the illegitimate African American daughter of Aaron Burr (1756-1836), who was a hero of the American Revolution, served as vice president under Thomas Jefferson, and took the life of Alexander Hamilton in a duel. Her mother was a Haitian woman named Eugenie. Her brother, John

Burr, a well-known barber and community leader, and his wife, Hetty, were notable station keepers on the Philadelphia Underground Railroad. Henrietta Bowers and Henrietta Clark were also known as tailoresses, as were Martha Montier, Sarah Eddy, Elizabeth Webb, Martha Gordon, and Sarah Shorter.

INTELLECTUAL AND LITERARY SOCIETY

In 1841, Joseph Willson's book *Sketches of The Higher Classes of Colored Society in Philadelphia* comprised one of the lengthiest and most important sources of the inner life of free northern African Americans prior to the Civil War. During the time the book was published, Philadelphia's colored population was estimated at 19,000. It was the largest and culturally the most significant of any urban community in the North.

Willson described parties, class attitudes, and cultural institutions of the African American elite. He wrote his book to combat prejudice from without and to correct abuses within the African American community. Throughout the years, Philadelphia intellectuals and fiery orators such as Russell Parrott, Hosea Easton, and Robert Purvis had called for stronger measures against racial prejudice and denial of civil liberties for African Americans. Four years before Joseph Willson wrote his book, Purvis had published his *Appeal of Forty Thousand Citizens Threatened with Disenfranchisement to the People of Pennsylvania* (1838). The Reform Convention in Pennsylvania "stripped us of a right (to vote), peaceably enjoyed during forty-seven years under the Constitution of this Commonwealth."

In 1829, David Walker, an African American free born, but the son of a slave father, hated slavery so intensely that he moved from Wilmington, North Carolina, to Boston. His famous pamphlet entitled *Walker's Appeal to the Colored People of the World*

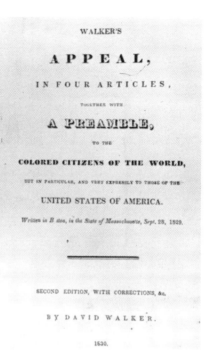

WALKER'S

APPEAL,

IN FOUR ARTICLES,

TOGETHER WITH

A PREAMBLE,

TO THE

COLORED CITIZENS OF THE WORLD,

BUT IN PARTICULAR, AND VERY EXPRESSLY TO THOSE OF THE

UNITED STATES OF AMERICA.

Written in B ston, in the State of Massachusetts, Sept. 28, 1829.

SECOND EDITION, WITH CORRECTIONS, &c.

BY DAVID WALKER.

1830.

*David Walker was born in Wilmington, North Carolina. Upon moving to
Boston, Massachusetts, he published his famous* Appeal in Four Articles.
*Within a year it went into three printings, greatly exciting all African Americans
who could read and infuriating the forces of slavocracy in the South.*

called for the elimination of slavery by any means necessary.
Within a year it went into three printings. Robert Roberts, another Boston African American, published a gentler book two years
earlier in 1827, *The House Servant Directory.* Roberts' book was
the first cookbook published in the United States by an African
American. His book was widely consulted by caterers in
Philadelphia and in other cities throughout the country.

TEN

OTHER CURIOUS PERSONS
AND JEWS WHO OWNED SLAVES

Francisco, a free person of African descent, was one of the 23 founders of
Bushwick in Brooklyn, New York. Known as "Francisco the Negro," he owned
a large amount of real estate.

$\mathcal{P}$eople of African descent were among the founding fathers and mothers during colonial America and during the era of the Revolutionary War. They were often respected as individuals. As the colonies grew into a nation, cheap labor was needed and they were reduced to the status of slaves.

Many free and enslaved African people were resourceful. Richard Johnson, who served as a faithful servant to Anthony Johnson, one of the 20 enslaved Africans who arrived in Virginia in 1619, was able to purchases two white servants of his own. His neighbor John Johnson, the son of Anthony, had imported 11 people white and black, and received 500 acres.

Free African people in New York were given equal opportunities with whites under the Dutch. "The Dutch blacks are very free and familiar," complained an English sea captain held prisoner in New Amsterdam (New York), "sauntering about among whites with hat on head and freely joining in conversations as if they were one and all of the same household."

TITUBA – THE BLACK WITCH OF SALEM

Until recent years, the true story of one of Colonial America's most famous personalities—Tituba the alleged Black witch of Salem, Massachusetts—had not been fully told. She was born on the Caribbean Island of Barbados, where the Reverend Samuel Parris purchased Tituba and her husband John and brought them to Salem to assist his ailing wife, his six-year-old daughter, and his wife's 19-year-old niece.

Reverend Parris occasionally hired Tituba and John out, assuring his family of extra income. During the long cold Salem winters, Tituba often entertained the children with stories about her life in Barbados. Her stories included tales of magic spells and her ability to read palms.

Gradually Tituba's fame spread throughout Salem Village, as witchcraft became a subject of conversation throughout the Massachusetts Bay Colony. Some of the young girls, including the children of Tituba's master, accused her of being a witch and telling them spellbinding tales. In 1692, Tituba and several other women were accused of being witches and sentenced to death.

The witchcraft scare continued for over a year and about 20 persons were hanged on Gallows Hill. Two other persons died in prison. Tituba insisted that she was not and never had been a witch. Finally, Tituba was released from prison and sold to another master. This enslaved woman who used the African art of healing to help her master's wife and others, became the catalyst of the most famous of the 17th-century witchcraft trials.

Among the people of African descent who achieved status in the Dutch controlled island was a freeman named Francisco Bastien, who in 1674 purchased four acres of land from the daughter of governor Peter Stuyvesant and later purchased 15 additional acres in 1684. "Francisco the Negro," as he was called, was one of 23 founders of Brooklyn.

Another New York resident, Jupiter Hammon, was largely ignored throughout the 19th century. Hammon, who was born in 1710, belonged to the prosperous New York slave-trading Lloyd family. Hammon was given opportunity for schooling and permitted to attend church. Hammon is important for one reason only: he was the first published African American lyric poet.

Preceding Phillis Wheatley by nearly 10 years, his first poem, *An Evening Thought Salvation by Christ with Penitential Cries*, was printed in 1760 as a broadside. His exceedingly rare poem *An Address to Miss Phillis Wheatley* appeared as a broadside in 1778. When he was 76 years old, Hammon published his address to the Negro in the State of New York not very far from the Samuel Fraunces Tavern in New York City.

Lucy Terry is credited as being the first person of African

descent to be called a poet, and one of America's earliest poets. Like Phillis Wheatley, she had been stolen from Africa as a young child and was baptized at the age of five in 1735. Lucy was 16 when she eye-witnessed a massacre by a party of Native Americans in the village of Deerfield, Massachusetts. She escaped. Later she wrote a rough-hewn ballad on the terrifying event called "Bars Fight," which was printed a century later. ("Bars" was a colonial word for meadow.)

Lucy's description of the massacre is said to be the most vivid account of that event. She died at the age of 91. Although Lucy Terry's name is recorded in history as the first African American poet, Phillis Wheatley is generally credited with the honor because of her book of poetry published in 1773.

Ira Aldridge, the first internationally known African American actor, performed at African Grove Theater. He was born in 1807. For 40 years, Aldridge performed as a star in all of the major Europeans cities. He appeared in *The Padlock* as the singing slave Mungo, and in other popular plays of the day. Othello was his most popular role, appearing with the famous Edmund Kean as Iago. Aldridge never returned to the United States. He died on tour in 1867 in Poland. In his honor, there is an Ira Aldridge Memorial Chair in the Shakespeare Memorial Theater at Stratford on Avon in England.

Even in athletics, African Americans won fame both at home and abroad. Tom Molineux, born a slave in Virginia, became the first boxing champion and the first American athlete to compete abroad. Molineux won fame in Europe when he fought 40 rounds with Tom Cribb in England in 1810.

In the Sedwick family plot in Stockbridge, Massachusetts, a stone marks a grave with the following inscription: Elizabeth Freeman known by the name of Mumbet died December 28, 1829. Her supposed age was eighty-five years, born a slave.

Mumbet, as Elizabeth was affectionately called, was born

about 1742. Her parents were natives of Africa. At an early age, she was purchased with her sister by Colonel John Ashley of Sheffield, Massachusetts. One day, her master struck her with a severe blow upon her face. Mumbet left Ashley's home and refused to return.

Ashley appealed to the court for the return of Mumbet. However, she asked Theodore Sedwick, a young lawyer of nearby Stockbridge, to represent her in court. She asked the attorney if she could not claim liberty under the law. Mumbet explained that the Bill of Rights said that all were born free and equal, and that she was not a dumb beast. She stated that she heard of the Bill of Rights while serving dinner to some gentlemen who were talking about the Bill of Rights and the new Constitution of Massachusetts.

Sedwick argued the case in the county court house in Great Barrington and won Mumbet's freedom. Her former master had to pay her 30 shillings, since Massachusetts had abolished slavery. Mumbet's husband died on the battlefield during the Revolutionary War and she, nearly 40 years old, was alone with one daughter in 1781.

In Boston, a woman known as Belinda, an African, at the age of three score and ten, on February 4, 1783, submitted to the Massachusetts General Court a personal plea for her freedom by signing her name with an "X." She described with anguish in her voice the horror of the slave ship she witnessed while being transported to America.

Seventy years had passed, but Belinda vividly remembered her survival in the "Ship of Sorrow." She said she was 12 years old and "enjoyed the fragrance of her native groves... when, in a sacred grove, with each hand in that of a parent, paying her devotions to the great Orisa, who made all things, an armed band of white men, driving many of her country men in chains, rushed into the hallow shades, and enslaved her."

Belinda said that in the ship 300 Africans in chains suffered the most excruciating torment, and some of them rejoiced that the pangs of death came like balm to their wounds. Belinda's master, Isaac Royall, had left the area and the aged Belinda who had served him her whole life and increased his wealth, was free, she explained, and she was left to starve. She eventually won her freedom.

Some historians stated that it is possible that poets Phillis Wheatley and Prince Hall, founder of the African American Masonic Lodge, were present in the Boston courtroom as Belinda pleaded her case. Four years later, *The American Museum*, a Philadelphia magazine, published Belinda's manuscript.

In April of that year, four courageous enslaved Africans signed a petition to the general court of Massachusetts expressing with magnetic words, "We expect great things from men who have made such a noble stand against the designs of their fellowmen to enslave them, their portraits are vivid in the text of their pleas." The enslaved Africans were referring to the white men who called for freedom during the Boston Massacre on March 5, 1770.

The Reverend Lemuel Haynes has been described as an octogenarian whose years had stretched from the French and Indian War to the presidency of Andrew Jackson. Haynes, who fought in the Revolutionary

Prince Hall was born in Barbados. After arriving in Massachusetts, Hall became a soap manufacturer. He served in the Revolutionary War for the American Forces. He later became an abolitionist and a minister and founded the first African American Masonic Lodge No.1 in Boston on July 2, 1776.

171

War at the Battle of Ticonderoga, was the first African American in the United States to serve as a minister for a white congregation, heading various churches in Vermont for more than 20 years.

He was born in 1753 at West Hartford, Connecticut, to a father of African descent and a white woman of respectable ancestry. In the early days of slavery, particularly in New England, some African peoples were permitted to attend white churches, like the Quaker Meeting House. But they were duly segregated with special seating assignments.

Moreover, African American religious rituals were forbidden and drums were outlawed, since drums could be used to send messages even in the presence of white people.

Amos Fortune was still a boy when he was brought to America. After serving several masters, Fortune saved enough money to purchase his freedom when he was 60 years old. In 1781, he moved from Woburn, Massachusetts, to Jaffery, New Hampshire, to establish a tannery business. By the age of 70, Fortune had become one of Jaffery's leading citizens.

In 1795, he founded the Jaffery Social Library. A New Hampshire State Historical Marker reads: "Buried behind Jaffery's colonial meeting house nearby is the grave of Amos Fortune, 1710-1801, African born slave who purchased his freedom, established a tannery and left funds for Jaffery's Church and Schools."

The Rev. Lemuel Hayes fought in the Revolutionary War's first battle at Lexington on April 19, 1775, answering Paul Revere's midnight call to arms. He served with Ethan Allen's Green Mountain Boys and later became the first African American minister to serve as a pastor in an all white church in America.

His second wife, Violit Baldwin, also is buried in the cemetery. Amos had purchased her freedom from her slave master. Artist Gilbert Stuart, America's first master of portraiture, received his first impression from drawing Neptune Thurston, a slave and expert coppersmith, employed in his master's New England copper shop. Thurston sketched likenesses on the heads of casks, according to Edward Peterson's *History of Rhode Island* (1853).

Another historical event connected with Massachusetts pertains to an enslaved African man whose heroic deed saved the white citizens of Taunton, and probably saved the Plymouth colony from a Native American massacre on July 11, 1676. Jethro heard the plan of attack while being held as a prisoner, managed to escape, and returned to warn the white colonists who rallied to defend the colony.

Another New England former slave's life story is told in *The Narrative of the Life and Adventures of Venture, A Native of Africa, But Resident above Sixty Years in the United States of America*, published in 1778. Venture Smith said, "I was born in Guinea Africa about the year 1720, and my father was named Saungm Furro Prince of Dukandara." Smith spent most of his life in Connecticut. He became a folk hero and stories of his life have been passed on until present times. Smith, a tall man apparently inherited the size and stature of his father, a king in West Africa.

Jean Baptise Point Du Sables' name is unfamiliar to most Americans. During the era of the Revolutionary War, he made a name for himself in the wilderness when Native Americans were present. He founded Chicago. Du Sable was born in Haiti, the son of a white planter and a free Haitian woman.

In what now is the City of Chicago, he operated a trading post and learned the language of the Native Americans and married a Native American woman in 1788. They had two children, Suzanne and Jean Baptiste, Jr. In 1800, Du Sable sold his Chicago property to a white trader for $1,200. There is a tradition among the Potawatomi Native Americans that "the first white man to settle in Chicago was a Negro."

Moreau de St. Mery was an early writer who was at least sympathetic to people of African descent. He gave reliable information in his writings, including his journal, which is one of the more important historical and literary works written on early Philadelphia.

He said, "Under the heading colored people of all ages and both sexes, I include all persons not white, but free and descended from the African race. The people of color live entirely among themselves without distinguishing mulattos, griffers, Negroes and quadroons, who are extremely rare. All colored women of Philadelphia dress well on Sundays, and wear chignons of white people's hair. Old Negresses have white people false hair, Negresses wear pink," Mery explains, "Nearly all colored people are poor and unhappy and obliged to work as servants. A white servant, no matter who, would consider it a dishonor to eat with colored people. The protection that the Quakers pretend to grant them is like all the acts of this sect, an ostentatious display of humility. It is a form of condescension which many business men use to their advantage." He noted that the Irish Catholic Church on South Sixth Street does not allow colored persons to be buried in its cemetery. "Colored burials are extremely decent," he concludes, "workmen do not want to accept them or let them become apprentices."

From the time when William Penn was present in the colony, Quakers and others used enslaved Africans to help build meetinghouses, churches, brick kilns, breweries, shops, wharves, roads, and all other "improvements," helping to create Penn's City of Brotherly Love from a wilderness into a major city known as the "Athens of America." Moreover many of these skilled trade persons passed their unpaid trades on to family members, who used these trades for many decades in Philadelphia and in other parts of

North America.

The free people of African descent valued their families. Enslaved African people also valued their love ones, but they found it difficult to keep them together as a unit. However, once freed, they could marry, choose their own names and name their own children, all of which gave them a sense of pride. A large number of free people of African descent owned houses and properties by accumulating wealth from various professions and trades.

Robert Montier, a refugee from St. Dominique, became a successful bottler of beer by 1806. Several members of his family married into the Bustill family who resided in Philadelphia and Montgomery Counties

White Indentured Servants and Black Slave Owners

The first enslaved people in the American colonies were not people of African ancestry, but Native Americans and White Europeans. In Virginia, white servitude was for a limited period, but was sometimes extended to life. Anthony Johnson was one of the original 20 Africans who had been brought to Jamestown, Virginia, as slaves in 1619.

Johnson, an indentured servant, was freed in 1622 or 1623, settled in Accomack County, was among the first African freedman and the first black landowner in the colonies. He went on to achieve another, though ignoble, African American first—the first black owner of slaves in the colonies. By 1651, Johnson was able to pay for the importation of five persons into Virginia for whose "head rights" he received 250 acres of land. That same year, he had been able to persuade the local court that he was entitled to receive services "for life" from John Casor, a black man. This decision marks the first time that a court decreed life servitude for any reason other than punishment for crime. Johnson's son, Richard, a large landowner himself, later brought 30 white indentured servants to work for him.

In 1625, there were reported to be in Virginia 464 white servants and only 22 Negroes. In the five years preceding, the number of Negroes had increased but two.

Before Europeans arrived in the American colonies, whites were in bondage in the West Indies. White men, women, and children were kidnapped in the British West Indies islands at the rate of several hundreds yearly in the 17th and 18th centuries and sold into slavery in America.

In 1670, Virginia passed a law forbidding African people and Native Americans from buying white people as slaves. This was 51 years after enslaved Africans arrived in Jamestown. In 1670, a Virginia law stated that "No Negro, mulatto, Indian, although a Christian or any Jew, Moor, Mohammedan…shall purchase any Christian white servants." White Europeans were sold in the United States up to 1826, 50 years after the signing of the Declaration of Independence. Even Andrew Johnson, President of the United States, was an indentured servant who ran away and was advertised for capture in the newspapers. George Bourne in his book *Picture of Slavery in the United States of America* (1834) states that white children were sometimes tanned to be sold as Negroes in the Deep South.

Freed African Americans bought white people in such numbers in Louisiana that a state law was passed in 1818 forbidding them from buying white people. One of the most notorious cases of a white person sold as a person of African descent was Salome, or Sally as she was called. She was born in Alsace, Germany, July 10, 1813, and was brought to America in 1817 by her father, who was to be sold into indentured servitude. On the voyage to America, her mother died and soon after arriving in America, her father died.

In the confusion of departure from the vessel, Sally was

separated from the rest of her family and fell into the hands of Fritz J. Miller, a slave trader. He specialized in the business of selling kidnapped white people as Negroes. Sally Muller was held in servitude in Louisiana for almost two years. Court after court ruled against her. Finally her birth certificate was located in Germany and the United States Supreme Court freed her in 1818.

Between 1526 and 1859 it is recorded that there were more than 33 major slave revolts in the United States. The Nat Turner Revolt of Virginia in 1831 is the most widely known. In Florida, the Seminoles, Native Americans, held whites as slaves and welcomed enslaved African runaways from Georgia and South Carolina as well as Florida who fled through swamps and wilderness into Seminole territory.

When the Seminoles were removed to Indian Territory starting in the early 1830s, 450 to 500 former enslaved Africans who had intermarried into the Seminole community went with them. In his book *White Servitude In Pennsylvania*, Chessman A. Herrick wrote, "No evidence is conclusive to show how early servile labor was introduced into Pennsylvania. A white servant was early brought to Delaware and was retained by Governor Printz on his Tinicum Island estate. Men described as the lowest class of the Swedes were to remain in slavery and were employed in digging earth, throwing up trenches and erecting walls and other fortifications."

William Penn on his first visit to his colony brought servants. Some 60 or 70 others were sent out to labor while his ship, the *Welcome*, was still out to sea. As indentured servants arrived in Pennsylvania, others were being received into New Jersey, Maryland, and Delaware. Demand for settlers created a demand for additional indentured servants. It was the Quaker majorities of the early colonial Pennsylvania Assemblies that passed restrictive measures to control white indentured servants and enslaved

African Americans.

One European traveler, Peter Kalm, commented on the scruples of Quakers, saying they were "no longer so nice" and that they had "as many Negroes as other people," but immediately following he remarked on the free Negroes who were lucky enough to have as masters some zealous Quakers. Some white citizens in Pennsylvania and in other colonies practiced voluntary servitude to pay off debts. Other servants ran away from their employers as indicated in the following advertisement from December 7, 1796:

Six Cent Reward – Philadelphia.

Ran away from the subscriber on the 21st of September, a bound girl named Sarah Newton, about seven years of age, fair complexion, black hair, and dark eyes; had on a stripped cotton short gown and brown petticoat when she went away. Whoever takes up said girl and brings her to me at No. 143 North Front Street, shall receive the above reward but no charges.

John Patterson

Germans and other member of the Lutheran Protestant denomination generally did not employ indentured servants or enslave Africans. As regards to the Irish, they were once highly scorned in America. Many of them arrived in this country as indentured servants, being mobbed, beaten, and refused work in most northern cities and towns.

Certain southern states such as Maryland placed a heavy tax on their entry. In Philadelphia, New York, and in certain states in New England, signs were placed on shops and other businesses that "No Irish need apply."

In 1844, Philadelphia became the site of the largest anti-

Irish riot in America where mobs fought them for four consecutive days. Some of the Irish became antagonistic against African Americans because both were competing for the same lowest paid jobs. However there was considerable marriage between African American men and Irish women.

David G. Croly wrote in his pamphlet *Miscegenation* (1864): Whenever there is a poor community of Irish in the North they usually herd with the poor Negroes and as a result of the various offices of kindness which only the poor can pay to one another, families become intermingled and concubine relations are formed between the black man and the white Irish women.

There are manumission papers and other documents by the hundreds among the records of the Pennsylvania Abolition Society, but few pertain to early African American ship builders.

The following document was sent by the Delaware Abolition Society to members of the Pennsylvania Abolition Society in 1787. This unique document provides detailed information regarding the maritime life of Gabriel Jackson ship builder.

> We the Subscribers after One Inquiry, and on our own knowledge. Respecting Gabriel Jackson, a Black man, (now living in the Borough of Wilmington Newcastle County, in the Delaware State) Do Report to Whom it may Concern as Follows viz. He was born the 16th day of the 5 month Domini 1734, on the plantation of Adam Buckley in the county aforesaid, and deemed the property of Susana Empson, who moved to Philadelphia when he said Gabriel was about 12 years old, where he was Learned to Read, Write & Cypher,

And put apprentice to William
Cunningham of the City of
Philadelphia aforesaid, to Learn the
Trade of Ship Building, and served Six
Years, and continued at his Trade
whereby he earned Considerable for
his said Mistress, who afterwards was
Married to Joshua North, of the said
City, who Hired the said Gabriel to
William Woodcock of the said
Borough of Wilmington, for several
years as a Journeyman Shipcarpenter,
and thereby procuring for (Domini
1765) his said Master Several
Hundred pounds; During which time,
the said Gabriel Married Brown Betty,
a poor industrious Girl, by whom he
has a Son named Gabriel, now a Ship
carpenter also. And we find the said
Joshua North for a Valuable
Consideration to him in Hand paid by
the said Betty Jackson, Did Release
the said Gabriel Jackson as by the said
Release Bearing Date the 20th of
September 1777, Fully appears.

We also find that the said Gabriel
Jackson is Legally seized and pos-
sessed of a Lot situate in the said
Borough of Wilmington + has
Erected two Tolerable Dwelling
Houses thereon, and hold
Considerable other property, which we
Believe they Have Acquired by the

Dint of Industry and Ingenuity, and that they live in Good repute amongst their Neighbors.

A Testimony of his the Said Gabriel Jacksons being a Master Workman at his Trade appears by his Building Several Sloops, and other vessels, without the projecting aid of any now in Occupation by their respective Owners, on Testimony of the above Tract we Subscribe Our hands this 16th day of the 10th month Dom 1787.

The deposition was signed by 43 prominent Wilmington, Delaware, white citizens, many of whom were connected in shipping and maritime commerce. The letter was sent to James Gibbons of the Pennsylvania Abolition Society.

REGISTER OF TRADES FOR PEOPLE OF AFRICAN DESCENT IN EARLY AMERICA

ashman

bakers

basket-makers

blacksmiths

barbers

bleeders

boot and shoemakers

book binders

brass founders

brewers

bricklayers

coachmen

brush makers

cabinet makers

caterers

carpenters

caulkers

chair maker

chimney sweepers

confectioners

cooks

coopers

coachmen

oystermen

curriers
ditch diggers
domestics
dyers
farmers
fishermen
fullers
glass makers
gardeners
grave diggers
grocers
hair dressers
hod carriers
hostess
laborers
matchmakers
mid-wife
ministers
musicians

plasterers
porters
rope maker
sail maker
seamen
ship carpenters
silversmiths
soap maker
stone cutter
tailors
tanners
tin plate workers
undertakers
venders
washer women
waiter
weaver
wheelwrights

WOMEN SLAVE OWNERS

It is wrong to believe that only men were slave owners; women also participated in ownership of enslaved people of African descent. Some women received slaves through inheritance as property from their parents or upon the death of their husbands, while others purchased slaves whenever it became necessary to acquire them.

Quaker Elizabeth Montgomery of Wilmington, Delaware, wrote in *Reminiscences of Wilmington in Familiar Village Tales Ancient and New* (1851), that in 1761 "a gang or drove of slaves, numbering twenty or thirty, was passing by my father's door."

Her mother purchased a nine-year-old boy from the group, who remained with the family for many years and was finally given his freedom.

The Pennsylvania Abolition Society Minute Book for May 29, 1775, records the case of Ann Humphries, a widow who claimed a slave by the name of Harry as her property. Harry stated that his master, Jonathan Humphries, had granted him his freedom and produced several witnesses to verify his case. He explained his situation to members of the Pennsylvania Abolition Society. Later Harry appealed his case before the Supreme Council, who demanded that the widow not sell Harry until the case was decided in court.

Ann Humphries defied the order and sold Harry to a captain of a sailing vessel, who locked Harry up until the captain could find a buyer. Harry eventually escaped his imprisonment and left with the British for New York in June 1778.

Slavery required unconditional submission. However, there is little doubt that Silvia Dubois possessed an indomitable spirit and was difficult to control. She was a powerful and incredibly long-lived woman born in Ringoes, New Jersey, in 1768. She said she "struck her (mistress) a hell of a blow with my fist." She lived for a time in Philadelphia, where her master owned a tavern. In 1883, her biographer, Cornelius Wilson Larison, published his book entitled *Silvia Dubois (now 116 years old) A Biography of the Slave who Whipt her Mistress and Granted her Freedom.* Like Black Alice of Dunks Ferry, Bucks County, Silvia represented the strength and stability of enslaved women who have a legion of stories to tell.

Another curious person of the time was a New York State slave named Isabella Baumfree, who shed her slave name and called herself Sojourner Truth. She was born about 1797, the property of a Dutch master. She spoke English with a Dutch accent all her life. One day in 1843, she decided to leave her job as a domestic servant to travel. "The Spirit calls me," she said, "and I must go." With only a few coins in her purse, Sojourner, despite her lack of education and training, began to speak out against slavery throughout the country.

With her six-foot frame and deep resonant voice, Truth aroused curiosity wherever she appeared. She is remembered for her famous speech "Ain't I a Woman?" delivered in Akron, Ohio, in 1851. Because of her eloquent speeches, she ranked only behind her friend Frederick Douglass and was invited to the White House by President Abraham Lincoln. Her friend Harriet Tubman was an even greater irritant to slave holders, than Sojourner, for not only did Tubman make speeches in the North, but also traveled on numerous occasions to bring enslaved men, women, and children out to freedom through the Underground Railroad, and never lost a passenger.

Patty Cannon, who lived along the Eastern Shore of Delaware and Maryland, not only kidnapped African American men, women, and children, but she ran her Underground Railroad in reverse. Her place of operation was located in Dorchester and Carolina counties, Maryland, and Sussex County, Delaware. Patty Cannon, a tall, white woman whose salty language was her trademark, and her merciless gang of kidnappers used this perilous

Sylvia Dubois, born a slave, lived in Philadelphia, Pennsylvania, and later in New Jersey. She is recorded in history as the slave who whipped her mistress. A book was written about her life. She died at the age of 116.

Sojourner Truth, standing six feet tall, a former New York slave, changed her slave name to Sojourner Truth. With her commanding voice and determined spirit, she became one of the leading orators of her day. In 1851 she delivered her "Ain't I a Woman" speech at the National Convention for Women Rights in Akron, Ohio.

location as a slave holding pen before they would sell their kidnapped captives to slave traders as far as New Orleans.

A letter to Philadelphia Mayor Joseph Watson in 1826 suggests that her gang was abducting blacks as far north as his city. Sometimes Patty Cannon employed renegade blacks to entice enslaved and free African people from the streets of Philadelphia and cities in New Jersey. Finally, captured and indicted for murder of four runaway slaves, two of them children, Patty Cannon poisoned herself on May 11, 1829, with her own foul hands in her cell in Georgetown, Delaware, cheating a public eager to witness her trial and execution.

JEWS WHO OWNED SLAVES

Jews invested heavily and became willing partners in purchasing and owning enslaved African people even during the Colonial period of North America, Central America, South America, and in the Caribbean Islands. This fact is confirmed by Jewish scholars and historians such as Solomon Grayzel, Henry L. Feingold, and others. Philadelphians Edwin Wolf II and Maxwell Whiteman wrote on Jews who participated in the unspeakable Holocaust that is human slavery. Philip D. Curtin, author of *The Atlantic Slave Trade* (1981), traced the most circulated slave importation figure to 15 million. Other scholars and historians estimated that the numbers were much higher.

The busy New England shipping centers of Bristol, Newport, and Providence, Rhode Island, dealt directly and indirectly in the Atlantic slave trade. Brown University in Providence, Rhode Island, was founded primarily by the wealth of the slave trading Brown family. Jewish bankers and shipping merchants in New York City, Charleston, South Carolina, and New Orleans were also directly or indirectly involved in slavery for profit.

In New Orleans, the notorious pirate of French and Jewish ancestry Jean Laffite was actively involved in the slave trade. His pirate empire spanned the entire Caribbean Island. Laffite once dispatched 60 vessels throughout the Caribbean to hunt a Spanish slave ship and proceeded to hold weekly slave auctions in the Louisiana coastal town of Barataria. During the War of 1812, Laffite assisted General Andrew Jackson win the Battle of New Orleans. About 200 of Jackson's soldiers were free African American riflemen who volunteered for the battle. Jackson praised them for their courage and loyalty.

A vast amount of Rhode Island's early wealth was accumulated from the slave trade, especially in Newport. It has been estimated that Rhode Island's slave trade employed 100-150 vessels annually carrying to Jamaica 80 to 100 enslaved African men, women and children in exchange for rum and other products from the lucrative slave trade.

PHILADELPHIA JEWS WHO OWNED SLAVES

History records that Robert Morris, Benjamin Franklin, and Jewish banker Haym Salomon did more than any other individuals to help finance the Revolutionary War. Salomon organized a brokerage firm in Philadelphia and the government borrowed more that $600,000 from him. He advanced other money to pay the salaries of government officials and agents of other countries and to outfit the troops during the Revolutionary War.

Salomon was associated in business with Robert Morris, a wealthy Quaker merchant and slave trader. Salomon owned a 20-year-old slave named Joe. After the war, he had business difficulties and died bankrupt, and his partner Robert Morris served time in debtor's prison for a short time.

Individual Jews had appeared in Philadelphia as early as 1703.

By 1738, several influential and wealthy families banded together to form a vibrant Jewish community. Jacob Franks, Joseph Simon, Nathan Levy, Solomon Etting, and the Gratz family participated in various forms of slavery. It is ironic that the firm of Levy, Franks and Simon (founded in 1751) represented the merchant conglomeration that owned Myrtilla the 250-ton, 10-gun vessel that brought the 2,000-pound Liberty Bell to Philadelphia. The Myrtilla left London some time after July 5, and arrived in Philadelphia about September 1. Because of the calendar change that took place at the time, the exact date remains undetermined. For many years, the Myrtilla was registered in the name of the notorious slave trading families of Levy and Franks in Philadelphia.

Nathan Levy with his brother Isaac many years earlier, on January 3, 1738, advertised in Benjamin Franklin's *Gazette* for buyers for "a likely young Negro man to be sold, fit for town and country."

Isaac Franks, a member of the conglomeration that owned the *Myrtilla*, once owned the Deshler-Morris House in Germantown. He leased it to President George Washington and his family during the yellow fever epidemic. Washington lived there for several weeks in November 1793. The President moved out of the house after having some difficulties with Franks about the rent and costs. However, he later returned in July 1794.

Franks sold slaves from time to time and owned a young female girl named "Belle." As early as January 4, 1786, Franks advertised in the *Pennsylvania Journal*: "For Sale. A Young likely Negro wench. About eight years old; has twenty years to serve."

Franks is said to had made his fortune in armaments and slaves during Queen Ann's War (1702-13), which gave Great Britain a monopoly in the slave trade. Isaac Levy operated in New York, Philadelphia, Boston, and London, and was part owner of the slave ship *Crown Gally*. Franks once brought 117 enslaved Africans into bondage.

Other Philadelphia slave traders and owners included

Samuel Hays, Israel Jacobs, Philip Moses Russell, Moses Myers, Isaac Frank, Bernard Gratz, Isaac Pesoa, Solomon Alexander, Solomon Moline, and Dr. David Nassy, whose family owned a large plantation in Surinam.

Jews had arrived in South America between 1639 and 1654 with a large number of slaves as sugar, coffee, cotton, and lumber workers. Nassy had arrived in Philadelphia escaping the Haitian revolt, where he had lived for several years. Levy Andrew and his wife Susannah owned an enslaved African girl whom they later took to Pittsburgh, a small village at that time. The Levys' slave is reported to have been one of the first people of African descent to settle in Pittsburgh.

Rabbi Jacob Cohen advertised in a Philadelphia newspaper that his bound girl ran away and offered an award of one dollar to anyone who would bring her home and take her to the gaol (jail.)

Lucy Marks, an enslaved African woman of the prominent Henry Marks family of Philadelphia, took her owner's surname, as was the common practice during the period of enslavement. According to Jewish historian Maxwell Whiteman, Lucy was a member of congregation Mikveh Israel in the 1790s and also a member of the Ladies of Mikveh Israel, observing the traditions of Judaism. Upon her death in 1823, the family applied for the customary burial in the cemetery. Some of the member of the congregation protested the burial of a servant in the synagogue's cemetery. After a short delay and intense support from other members, Lucy was buried in an unmarked grave near the entrance of the cemetery.

Rebecca Gratz, the inspiration for a character in Sir Walter Scott's *Ivanhoe*, in attempting to have her non-Jewish mother buried in the same cemetery, used the fact of Lucy Marks' grave to illustrate that the cemetery already received a non-Jew and the privilege should be extended to her parents. Rebecca Gratz was unsuccessful in changing the rules of Milkveh Israel cemetery.

Senator James Buchanan presented a memorial from 24 Jews of Philadelphia in favor of the abolition of slavery in the District of Columbia. Other members of Philadelphia's Jewish community participated in the anti-slavery movement. When the Pennsylvania Abolition Society reorganized in 1787, several Jews were among the society's members. Benjamin Nones was one of the most active members of the Society, encouraging other Philadelphia Jews to free their slaves immediately. Nones also shared his abolition commitment with Cyrus Bustill, the respected African American leader.

THE BURNING OF AFRICAN AMERICANS AT THE STAKE

If enslaved and freed people of African descent were important factors in the economic well-being of colonial and revolutionary America, they were often regarded as outcasts politically and socially. Indeed, almost without exception each colony had its system of control for African people; their harshness and severity generally depended upon the ratio of African people in their population.

For instance, in New York, 50 years after the witch hunt at Salem, Massachusetts, a hunt of a different color occurred. By the time it was over, four whites and 13 persons of African descent had been burned, 18 African persons had been hanged, and 70 more had been deported. It started on March 14, 1741, when several buildings were set ablaze and African people were seen in the vicinity of the fires.

Through the testimony of several informers, including one woman so brazen a liar that the authorities eventually disregarded her stories, almost 200 people were implicated in a conspiracy. The history of the plot was recorded in Daniel Horsmanden's *A*

Quaco, accused leader of the New York City conspiracy trails, was burned at the stake in 1741. The alleged conspiracy accused a slave of setting a fire that caused damage to the governor's mansion and destroyed a church and also of taking part in the "Negro plot." More than 150 persons of African descent were arrested during the investigation. Between May 11 and August 29, 31 persons of African descent and four whites were executed for their alleged role in the conspiracy. Eighteen African persons, two white men and two white women were also hanged. Seventy Africans were transported out of New York.

Journal of the Proceedings in the Detection of the Conspiracy Formed by some White People in Conjunction with Negroes and other Slaves for Burning the City of New York in America. The book was published in 1744. Shortly after this horrifying event, free and enslaved African people throughout the colonies had to have a pass in order to travel. They were segregated in public and socially ostracized in private.

MAINE'S AFRICAN AMERICAN PIONEERS

The presence of African Americans in Maine as a subject for scholarly examination is a field untouched until recent years and is only now undergoing scrutiny. Early records reveal that people of African descent arrived in Maine from Cape de Verde, an island off of West Africa that was the home of fishermen who fished the Atlantic Ocean since the 1500s. Many of these sailors and fishermen settled in Maine after the Revolutionary War.

Married in 1783 in New Gloucestor, Boston and Zeruiah Lewis, husband and wife, are reported to have been among the first African Americans to settle in Maine. Born in 1798, Reuben Ruby and five other African Americans in Portland publicly condemned white churches that excluded people of African descent in 1826. Ruby also was active in the formation of the Abyssinian Religious Society (1828) and helped to incorporate the Maine Anti-Slavery Society in 1834. He was also connected with Portland's Abyssinian Meetinghouse, an African American church that was one of many places in Maine that harbored escapees on the Underground Railroad network. Maine was a pivotal junction point on the railroad due to its location near Canada.

Another African American, John Brown Russworn, born in 1799, in Port Antonio, Jamaica, spent some of his growing up years in Portland and was the first African American graduate of

Bowdoin College in 1826. Russworn was the third African American to graduate from an American college. With Samuel Cornish as senior editor, Russworn became an editor of *Freedom's Journal*, the first African American newspaper in 1827. Russworn was also noted for his abolitionist views against slavery. He emigrated to Liberia in West Africa and eventually became its first black governor of the colony of Maryland, now a part of Liberia, where he is buried.

Another African American, James Augustine Healy, was the first African American Catholic bishop in the nation. While living in Maine, Healy became bishop of the diocese of Portland from 1875 to 1900. Macon Bolling Allen was the first African American to be licensed to practice law, accepted to the bar in 1844, in Portland. Allen later practiced law in Massachusetts, South Carolina, and Washington, D.C.

A CHRONOLOGY OF AFRICAN AMERICAN PARTICIPATION IN THE ERA OF THE REVOLUTION

1770, March 5 – British troops open fire on a crowd of protestors apparently led by runaway slave Crispus Attucks; Attucks is the first of five patriots to die for freedom in what history remembers as the Boston Massacre.

1772, June 9 – An African American man named Arron Briggs participates in the burning of the British revenue cutter *Gaspee* off the coast of Rhode Island.

1773, July 5 – The Lord Mayor of London presents a copy of *Paradise Lost* to Phillis Wheatley, the black American poet. Wheatley, who gained her freedom in 1771, published her first book of poetry. Her poems were admired by John Paul Jones, father of the American Navy, and by General George Washington.

1773, **November** – Massachusetts slave Caesar Hendricks takes his master to court "for detaining him in slavery." An all-white jury frees Hendricks and awards him damages.

1774, **September 7** – Abigail Adams, in a letter to her husband, John, writes: "It always appeared a most iniquitous scheme to me to fight ourselves for what we are daily robbing and plundering from those who have as good a right to freedom as we have."

1774, **October 2** – The Continental Congress votes for discontinuance of the slave trade after December 1, 1774.

1775, **March 8** – Thomas Paine publishes his first essay, "African Slavery in America," which denounces slavery, calls for abolition, and demands that blacks be given land in payment for long years of slavery.

1775, **March 10** – Daniel Boone's expedition sets out for Kentucky guided by an aged African American man.

1775, **April 18** – The midnight rides of Paul Revere and William Dawes alert the Minutemen, many of whom were African Americans volunteers, that the British are coming

1775, **April 19** – Black American Minutemen fighting in the first battles of the Revolution at Lexington and Concord include Peter Salem, Lemuel Haynes, Pompy, Prince, Prince Estabrook (wounded), Pomp Blackman (at both battles), Cato Stedman, Cato Boardman, Cuff Whitmore, and Cato Wood.

1775, **May 1** – Lemuel Haynes and two other African American volunteers in Ethan Allen's Green Mountain Boys take part in America's first aggressive military action, the capture of Fort Ticonderoga.

1775, **July 3** – Prince Hall founds the first lodge of African American Free Masons in Boston.

1775, **November 7** – The Earl of Dunmore, Virginia's royal governor, issues his famous proclamation offering freedom to slaves who will desert their rebel masters and join the British army.

1775, **December 5** – Salem Poor's extraordinary bravery at the battle of Bunker Hill is praised by 14 officers who send a petition on his behalf to the General Court of Massachusetts.

1776, **January 1** – Gen. Washington writes to John Hancock, president of the Continental Congress, to press for a decision allowing the enlistment of free black soldiers.

1776, **February 28** – Gen. Washington invites poet Phillis Wheatley to his Cambridge headquarters to thank her for a poem in his honor.

1776, **April** – South Carolina authorizes the death penalty for slaves who defect to join the British.

1776, **April 6** – Congress bans the importation of slaves into the thirteen colonies.

1776, **April 23** – To prevent black defections to the British force in the area of Charleston, S.C., General R.H. Lee orders all blacks who can fight to be "secured immediately and sent up to Norfolk."

1776, June – Virginia navy pilot Minny, a slave volunteer, is killed attempting to board an enemy vessel in the Rappahannock River

1776, June 17 – Thomas Hickey is hanged for conspiracy against Gen. Washington, after his plot was exposed by African American serving girl Phoebe Fraunces.

1776, July 4 – The Declaration of Independence is adopted in Philadelphia, but only after voting out Thomas Jefferson's sharp condemnation of the slave trade as "cruel war against human nature itself, violating its most sacred rights of life and liberty."

1776, September 22 - The British hang Nathan Hale as an American spy; the hangman is 15-year-old loyalist slave Bill Richmond, who in later years becomes Europe's heavyweight boxing champion.

1776, December 25 – Washington makes his famous midnight crossing of the icy Delaware River; many black soldiers are in the boats, including Prince Whipple and Oliver Cromwell.

1777 – Cato Carlile and Scipio Africanus, freeborn blacks from New England coastal towns, enlist for service under Capt. John Paul Jones; the navy welcomes black men who know the sea, whether they be free or slave.

1777, October 23 – A Hessian officer's diary reads, "The Negro can take the field instead of his master, and therefore no regiment is to be seen in which there are not Negroes in abundance, and among them are able-bodied and strong fellows."

1777, November 15 – The Articles of Confederation, which govern the states during the Revolution, are adopted; the document makes no reference to black people.

1777, **December 11** – Washington begins his retreat to Valley Forge; many soldiers will desert during this terrible winter, but black troops less than whites.

1778, **January 1** – Rhode Island's two battalions are severely depleted at Valley Forge; General James Varnum proposes to Washington that the state be allowed to meet its quota by raising a slave-soldier regiment, and Washington agrees.

1778, **December 29** – The British capture Savannah, Ga., thanks to aged slave guide Quamino Dolly, who volunteers to lead them through a heavy swamp to the undefended rear of the American position.

1779, **March 14** – Alexander Hamilton urges Congress to allow slaves to enlist, reminding them that "the contempt we have been taught to entertain for the blacks, makes us fancy many things that are founded neither in reason nor experience."

1779, **March 29** – Congress urges South Carolina and Georgia to immediately enlist 3,000 black soldiers; this so incenses the privy council of South Carolina that it recommends withdrawing from the Revolution.

This monument to African American soliders in the Revolutionary War is in Valley Forge National Historic Park

1779, July 15 – Black spy Pompey brings the information that Gen. Anthony Wayne uses to storm Stony Point, N.Y.

1779, September 23 - The Father of the American Navy, John Paul Jones in the *Bonhomme Richard,* whose crew includes free black seamen, defeats the *Serapis* in the Atlantic.

1779, October 9 – Count D'Estaing's 3,600-strong army, including 545 black troops from Santo Domingo, is beaten back from an ill-advised attack on Savannah, but the black unit holds off a British counterattack, preventing a rout.

1779, November 12 – African Americans petition the New Hampshire legislature to outlaw slavery.

1779, December 9 – Eighteen year old Jabez Jolly enlists in Capt. Rufus Lincoln's company of the 7th Mass. Regiment as a drummer, a typical assignment of African American soldiers.

1780, March 1 – Pennsylvania becomes the first state to pass a measure abolishing slavery; emancipation is to be gradual.

1780, October — Maryland authorizes slave enlistments, the only Southern state to do so during the Revolutionary War.

1781 — James Forten, not yet 15 years old, enlists as a powder-boy on the Pennsylvania privateer *Royal Lewis.*

1781, March 27 – General Lafayette takes James Armistead, an African American soldier, into his service as a spy.

1781, June – Virginia slave Saul Matthews, an American spy, returns with crucial information about British defenses and that very night leads the successful raid that forces Cornwallis to abandon his strong position at Portsmouth, Va.

1781, October 22 – Visiting Lafayette's camp, defeated Gen. Cornwallis is surprised to find that his chief black spy is really an American double agent; although unidentified, the black man is probably James Armistead.

1782, December 16 – The British evacuation of Charleston, S.C., is completed; 5, 327 escaped slaves leave with them to be resettled in Jamaica, St. Lucia, Halifax, East Florida, and England.

1783, April 19 – War is over. Congress declares more than 5,000 blacks have served in the American forces, and another 1,000 have borne arms for the British.

1783, December 4 – For his retirement banquet and farewell to his officers, Gen. Washington chooses New York City's Fraunces Tavern, a famous African American- owned restaurant.

Historians estimate that between 8,000 and 10,000 soldiers and sailors of African descent served in the American Continental, the British, and the Haitian armies during the Revolutionary War.

James Armistead, a Virginia slave, served with General Lafayette during the Revolution and won the trust of British General Cornwallis. As a spy for General George Washington, Armistead provided valuable information for the Continental Army.

SELECTED BIBLIOGRAPHY

Aptheker, Herbert, *The Negro in the American Revolution*, International Publishers, New York, 1940.

Ballard, Allen, B., *One More Day's Journey*, New York, McGraw Hill Book Company, 1984.

Bennett, Lerone, Jr., *Pioneers in Protest*, Johnson Publishing Co., Inc. Chicago, 1968.

Blassingame, John, W., *Black New Orleans, 1860-1880*, The University of Chicago Press, Chicago and London, 1973.

Blockson, Charles, L., *Pennsylvania's Black History*, Philadelphia Portfolio Associates, Inc. 1975.

Blockson, Charles, L., *African Americans in Pennsylvania, Above Ground and Underground*, R. B. Books, Harrisburg, 2001.

Branagan, Thomas, *Serious Remonstrances, Addressed to the Citizens of the Northern States and their Representatives.* Philadelphia, 1805.

Brown, William Wells, *The Black Man: His Antecedents: His Genius and His Achievements*, Thomas Hanulton, New York, 1863,

Cromwell, John W., *The Negro in American History: Men and Women Eminent in the Evolution of the Americans of African Descent*, Johnson Reprint Corporation, New York, 1968.

Dubois, W.E.Burghardt, Ph.D. *The Philadelphia Negro: A Social Study*, Ginn and Company, Boston, 1899.

Gibson, J.W. and Grogman, W. H., Progress of a Race, J.L. Nicholas and Company, Atlanta, 1902.

Hartgrove, W.B. "The Negro Soldier in the American Revolution," Journal of Negro History, 1:2 (April, 1916) 110-131.

Herrick, Cheesman, A., *White Servitude In Pennsylvania*, John Joseph McVey Co, Philadelphia, 1926.

Jensen, Arthur, *The Maritime Commerce of Philadelphia*, Society Press, Philadelphia, 1963.

Jordan, John Woolf, *Colonial and Revolutionary Families of Pennsylvania*, Lewis Publications, Philadelphia, 1911.

Jordan, Winthrop, D., *White Over Black; American Attitudes Toward the Negro 1550-1812*, University of North Carolina Press, Chapel Hill, 1968.

Jones, Absalom and Richard Allen, *A Narrative of the Proceedings of the Black People During the Late Awful Calamity in Philadelphia in the Year 1793: and the Refutation of Some Censures, Thrown Upon Them in Some Late Publications*, William W. Woodward, Philadelphia, 1794.

Kaplan, Sidney, *The Black Presence in the Era of the American Revolution: 1770-1800*, Graphic Society Ltd. in association with the Smithsonian Institution Press, New York, 1973.

Kelley, Joseph, J., Jr. *Life and Times in Colonial Philadelphia*, Stackpole Books Company, Harrisburg, 1973.

Lane, Roger. *William Dorsey's Philadelphia and Ours*, Oxford University Press, New York, 1992.

Lapsansky, Emma J., "Since They Got Those Separate Churches: Afro Americans and Racism in Jacksonian Philadelphia," *American Quarterly*, 32 (spring 1980) 54-78.

The Liberty Bell. Friends of Freedom, Boston, 1839.

Meltzer, Milton, ed., *In Their Own Words: A History of the American Negro, 1619 – 1865*, Thomas Y. Crowell Company, New York, 1964.

Nash, Gary B., "Slave and Slave Owners in Colonial Philadelphia," *William and Mary Quarterly*, (April 1973), 233-256.

Nash, Gary B. and Jean R. Soderlund, *Freedom by Degrees: Emancipation in Pennsylvania and Its Aftermath*, Oxford University Press, New York, 1991.

Nell, William, C., *The Colored Patriots of the American Revolution*, Boston, 1855.

Nell, William C., *Nineteenth Century African American Abolitionist, Historian, Internationalist Selected Writings 1832-1874*, Edited by Dorothy Porter Wesley and Constance Porter Uzelac, Black Classic Press, Baltimore, 2002.

Newman, Debra L., "Black Women in the Era of the American Revolution in Pennsylvania," *Journal of Negro History*, 61 (July 1976) 276-89.

Pipkin, Rev. J.J., *The Story of a Rising Race*, N.D. Thompson Publishing Company, New York, 1902.

Porter, Dorothy B., *Early Negro Writings: 1760-1837*, Beacon Press, Boston, 1971.

Powell, John H., *Bring Out Your Dead: The Great Plague of Yellow Fever in Philadelphia in 1793*, University of Pennsylvania Press, Philadelphia, 1949.

Quarles, Benjamin, *The Negro in the American Revolution*, University of North Carolina Press, 1961.

Quarles, Benjamin, *Black Abolitionists*, Oxford University Press, 1969.

Rogers, Joel, A., *Africa's Gift to America*, Futuro Press, Inc. New York, 1959.

Scharf, J. Thomas and Thompson Westcott, *History of Philadelphia 1639 – 1884*, L.H. Everts, 1884.

Simmons, William J., *Men of Mark: Eminent, Progressive and Rising*, W.W. Williams Co., Cleveland, 1887.

St. Mery, de Moreau, *Moreau de St. Mery's American Journal 1793-1798*, Translated and Edited by Kenneth Roberts and Anna M. Roberts, Doubleday and Company, Inc. New York, 1947.

Schomburg Center for Research in Black Culture, *The Black New Yorker. The Schomburg Illustrated Chronology*, written by Howard Dodson, Christopher Moore and Roberta Yancy, John Wiley and Sons, Inc. New York, 2000.

Smith, Billy G., ed., *Life in Early Philadelphia. Documents from the Revolutionary and Early National Periods*, The Pennsylvania State University Press, University Park, 1995.

Tinkcom, Harry M., "The Revolutionary City, 1765-1783," In Russell F. Weigley, ed. *Philadelphia – A 300 Year History*, W.W. Norton, New York, 1982.

Wax, Donald D., "Pennsylvania, Quaker Merchants and the Slave Trade in Colonial Pennsylvania," *Magazine of History and Biography*, Vol. 86, 1962.

Whiteman, Maxwell, *The Kidnapped and the Ransomed: The Narrative of Peter and Vina Still After Forty Years of Slavery with an Introductory Essay on Jews in the Anti-slavery Movement*, Jewish Publication Society, Philadelphia, 1970.

Whiteman, Maxwell. *The History of the Jews of Philadelphia*, Edited by Edwin Wolf, The Jewish Publication Society of America, Philadelphia, 1975.

Wildes, Harry Emerson, *Lonely Midas: The Story of Stephen Girard*, Farrar and Rinehart, Inc., New York, 1943.

Winch, Julie, *A Gentleman of Color- The Life of James Forten*, Oxford University Press, New York, 2002.

INDEX

Page numbers of illustrations are in **bold type.**

*The portraits on the cover include,
left to right, Reverend Peter Williams, Evangelist Juliann Jane Till-
mand and Cinque-African leader of
the Amistead revolt.*